RETIREMENT MIGRATION AND PRECARITY IN LATER LIFE

Marion Repetti and Toni Calasanti

First published in Great Britain in 2025 by

Policy Press, an imprint of
Bristol University Press
University of Bristol
1-9 Old Park Hill
Bristol
BS2 8BB
UK
t: +44 (0)117 374 6645
e: bup-info@bristol.ac.uk

Details of international sales and distribution partners are available at
policy.bristoluniversitypress.co.uk

© Bristol University Press 2025

British Library Cataloguing in Publication Data
A catalogue record for this book is available from the British Library

ISBN 978-1-4473-5821-3 hardcover
ISBN 978-1-4473-5822-0 paperback
ISBN 978-1-4473-5823-7 ePub
ISBN 978-1-4473-5824-4 ePdf

The right of Marion Repetti and Toni Calasanti to be identified as authors of this work has been asserted by them in accordance with the Copyright, Designs and Patents Act 1988.

All rights reserved: no part of this publication may be reproduced, stored in a retrieval system, or transmitted in any form or by any means, electronic, mechanical, photocopying, recording, or otherwise without the prior permission of Bristol University Press.

Every reasonable effort has been made to obtain permission to reproduce copyrighted material. If, however, anyone knows of an oversight, please contact the publisher.

The statements and opinions contained within this publication are solely those of the authors and not of the University of Bristol or Bristol University Press. The University of Bristol and Bristol University Press disclaim responsibility for any injury to persons or property resulting from any material published in this publication.

Bristol University Press and Policy Press work to counter discrimination on
grounds of gender, race, disability, age and sexuality.

Cover design: Bristol University Press
Front cover image: FreeImages/ Ayla87

Contents

Series editors' preface		iv
List of tables		vi
Acknowledgements		vii
1	Introduction	1
2	Retirement migration	13
3	Precarity and the welfare state in home and host countries	28
4	Escaping economic precarity	46
5	Escaping ageism	67
6	Relying on global privileges	89
7	Health and assistance precarity in later life	104
8	Retirement migration, precarity and age	118
Notes		131
References		132
Index		146

Series editors' preface

Chris Phillipson (University of Manchester, UK)
Toni Calasanti (Virginia Tech, USA)
Thomas Scharf (University of Newcastle, UK)

As the global older population continues to expand, new issues and concerns arise for consideration by academics, policy makers and practitioners worldwide. *Ageing in a Global Context* is a series of books, published by Policy Press in association with the British Society of Gerontology, which aims to influence and transform debates in what has become a fast-moving field in research and policy. The series seeks to achieve this in three main ways. First, the series publishes books that rethink key questions shaping debates in the study of ageing. This has become especially important given the restructuring of welfare states, alongside the complex nature of population change, with both of these elements opening up the need to explore themes that go beyond traditional perspectives in social gerontology. Second, the series represents a response to the impact of globalisation and related processes that are contributing to the erosion of the national boundaries that originally framed the study of ageing. From this has come the emergence of issues explored in various contributions to the series, for example: the impact of cultural diversity; changing patterns of working life; new forms of inequality; the role of ethnicity in later life; and related concerns. Third, a key concern of the series is to explore interdisciplinary connections in gerontology. Contributions to the series provide a critical assessment of the disciplinary boundaries and territories influencing later life, creating, in the process, new perspectives and approaches relevant to the 21st century.

Given the context described, *Retirement Migration and Precarity in Later Life* corresponds closely to the aims of the *Ageing in a Global Context* series. The issue of retirement migration has been a significant theme in research on ageing since at least the 1990s. Much of this work has tended towards presenting older migrants as an economically secure group seeking a leisure-based lifestyle as they transition from work to retirement. However, the authors provide a convincing challenge to this view, demonstrating the extent to which international migration among older people may be linked to the need to escape poverty and insecurity in their home country. Drawing upon fascinating interview material with retirees from the UK, the US and Switzerland, the book explores migration in the context of the ways in which precarity linked with ageism shapes the lives of older people. The book also provides unique insights into the various inequalities that shape interactions between migrants and the population of the communities into which they have moved. The study represents a major contribution to an important area of work in the field of ageing. It should attract an extensive readership, highlighting as it does significant cultural, economic and social changes affecting older people in the 21st century.

List of tables

2.1	Demographic profile of the interviewees	25
3.1	Income sources of older people and poverty rate	31
3.2	Differences and similarities in retirement and healthcare policies in the UK, Switzerland and the US (2020)	40
3.3	Swiss, UK and US retirement migrants' access to welfare state policies in Spain, Costa Rica and Mexico	43

Acknowledgements

In writing this book, we have benefited from the support of several colleagues and friends, as well as research institutions, to whom we would like to express our thanks. Laura Vickers-Rendall at Policy Press, as well as Jay Allan, provided helpful feedback and kept us on track, as did series editors Chris Phillipson and Thomas Scharf. Our book was also improved by the close reading and constructive suggestions of the anonymous reviewer. We are grateful to Neal King, who gave freely of his intellectual expertise, editorial suggestions and support throughout this work. We appreciate the work of Sadie Giles, whose help with the coding and analysis of the data enabled us to push this project forward more quickly than would otherwise have been the case. In addition, we are grateful to Jonathan Gehri Repetti for his support and care over the course of this work. We thank the Swiss National Science Foundation for awarding two postdoctoral fellowships and a mobility grant to the first author to conduct this research in Spain and Costa Rica and to write this book, and the College of Liberal Arts and Human Sciences at Virginia Tech for the travel and transcription support provided to the second author. Finally, and especially, we warmly thank all the people who agreed to participate in our research and trusted us with their stories.

1

Introduction

On 14 July 2022, International Living, a well-known company promoting international retirement migration,[1] posted to its website the testimony of John, an American retiree living in Costa Rica. John explains why he and his partner retired abroad:

> I grew up poor. I was the first person in the family to ever graduate college. I went on to become a physician and then returned to my hometown [and] had a successful career. You know – The American Dream. But somewhere along the way, [it] turned into An American Nightmare. Striving to achieve and maintain all that 'success' created consequences that demanded more and more of me. … That successful American dream was killing me. So, my partner … and I decided to look elsewhere for our dream. A dream that would let us slow down and enjoy life. (International Living, 2022)

John describes the better quality of his new life in Costa Rica:

> We live in an almost-secret valley at 4,000 feet elevation. Here we have no need of air conditioning or heating as our days average in the mid to upper 70s F. … The fertile, volcanic soils allow me to grow wonderful gardens of all kinds. … Between leaving the stress behind, walking much more, and living a generally more healthy lifestyle, I don't need to take blood pressure or cholesterol medicines anymore. … Because there are so many natural wonders to experience in this tiny country, we can take mini-vacations on a whim. And we have also taken several world vacations we would never have been able to do before due to time and money. … Property taxes are almost nothing. Private medical and dental care is about 1/4 to 1/3 of what it costs in the States. We live on about 1/3 of what we spent before we moved. Plus, now we have a maid twice a week, a full-time gardener, and a full-time handyman. We have plenty of time to socialize with friends again. … And speaking of friends, those who visit us from the States – the ones who thought we were nuts for moving – always comment on how happy, relaxed, and healthy we are. So, closing that door on an old

life and starting a new one here has been the best decision we ever made. (International Living, 2022)

Like John, many of the retirement migrants we met as we researched this book improved their quality of lives by relocating abroad. However, and in contrast to John's story, some of these retirees knew precarity before they moved. Their migration did not proceed from a position of relative comfort to seek a preferred lifestyle, but was primarily concerned with overcoming their tenuous economic situations. Stephanie provides one such example. She moved to Spain from the UK, where she was no longer employed and was too young to collect retirement benefits. Her living conditions in the UK were dire. She received disability benefits from the British state, but those were inadequate, and she struggled to pay for housing, food and energy costs. She lived with her mother and adult children; they sometimes suffered in cold weather because, "In the winters, the heating is very, very expensive, and mum and I would have one room that we would keep warm. And even with that, it was difficult to pay the bills." She also experienced hunger despite the food support that she received from the state. As soon as her children became independent, and when her mother moved into a nursing home, she moved to Spain. The cheaper cost of living, as well as the warmer climate and reduced need for heating, significantly improved her situation. Yet, this state of affairs was not secure in the long run, as she still lacked enough money and needed financial support from a male partner, who lived elsewhere. Without this help, she could not afford to live in Spain either.

This book aims to understand the motivations and experiences of international retirement migrants from Europe and North America, and to examine the role of precarity in later life in shaping this trend. In this first chapter, we position retirement migration within the larger context of international migration trends, outline the theoretical framework that we use in our examination of retirement migration and provide an overview of the chapters.

Retirement migration: a growing phenomenon

Over the last decade, the percentage of international migrants – people living in a country different than the one in which they were born – rose from 2.3 per cent in 1980 to 3.5 per cent in 2019 (UN, 2022). Typically, migrants move from a poorer country to one that is richer, often in the Global North, to find better work opportunities (Castles et al, 2014; Gatrell, 2019; Shah, 2020). Most of them are relatively young, with the mean age ranging from 38 in 1990 to 40 in 2019.[2]

Although it is not common among the majority of older people, migration also occurs among this group. International Organisation for Migration

(IOM, 2020) data for 2019 finds that 11.8 per cent of all the 'international migrant stock' (that is, foreign-born residents in a country, regardless of when they entered the country) were aged 65 and over, a percentage that has been relatively stable over the last 30 years. Most of them moved to a richer country for economic reasons, as noted earlier, and then age in place; others left their home country in later life to join their adult children who had migrated (Torres, 2012).

Retirement migration involves an opposite trend: the relocation of retirees from the Global North to countries with lower costs of living, a movement not linked to work opportunities. As it is less frequent and does not fit normative representations of major migration trends, this kind of later-life relocation raises such questions as: why do some retirees leave their richer country for a poorer one? What motivates this movement? How do they experience their migration?

As we will discuss, the first wave of scholarship often linked retirement migration to 'lifestyle'- or 'amenity'-related motivations, that is, retirees using their economic power in a poorer country to engage in leisure activities and consumption practices that they feel better reflects their tastes (King et al, 2019, 2000; Williams et al, 2000). This vision dovetails with the testimony of John, quoted earlier, and in the many contemporary advertisements for retirement migration appearing both in print and online, such as in the following typical promotion by International Living (no date) targeting North Americans:

> When you make the decision to retire to Mexico, you … don't have to choose between water or mountains; here, you can have them both at the same time. … You can … own the home of your dreams … for much less than it would cost you most anywhere in the U.S. or Canada. The real estate market offers endless possibilities. … You can buy land and build the house you always wanted to own, you can … retire on the … beachfront, on a golf course … the possibilities are virtually limitless. In fact, you could even retire on a ranch … if that's what your heart desires. Whether your vision of the ideal retirement involves shopping, fishing, sunbathing, diving, biking, mountain climbing, parasailing, collecting crafts, visiting archaeological sites, partying, going to concerts, attending the theatre, or fine dining, in Mexico you can engage in all these activities and many more.

Some scholars demonstrate that such capacity to maintain or improve a lifestyle in a poorer country relies on privileges derived from power relations between the Global North and South. Along these lines, they sometimes use the term 'expats', to highlight retirement migrants' social and economic power in contrast to that possessed by South – North migrants (see, for example, Lardiés-Bosque et al, 2016; Ciafone, 2017; Barbosa et al, 2021; Croucher, 2022). Migrants from the Global South are perceived as suspect in the Global North, whereas retirement migrants from the North do not encounter the same negative depiction in the South. However, using the term 'expat' tends to obscure the reality that these retirees are, in fact, migrants and the difference in their welcome (Hayes, 2018a); it is not merely international relocation that influences how migrants are treated. Thus, to avoid this obfuscation, we refer to 'expats' only when our interviewees use that term.

As a research arena, international retirement migration has developed further, maturing in light of both world events and scholarly findings. Scholars have increasingly pointed to the class dynamic at the heart of the noted quest for lifestyle retirement migration (see, for example, O'Reilly, 2007; Hall and Hardill, 2016; Botterill, 2017) and have acknowledged the economic precarity of some migrants (see Chapter 2), but the latter has rarely been the focus of research. However, the impact of recent global economic events and welfare state retrenchment encourages greater attention to, and centring upon, those retirement migrants who are precarious. In this regard, our data offer a view of retirement migration that differs from that literature that posits retirees from the Global North as carefree tourists and migrants who can use their privileges to pursue new adventures in the South. In line with some of the most recent scholarship (see Chapter 2), we illuminate the links between retirement migration and the precarity that can shape later life. Adding to this nascent literature, we delineate different forms of precarity and how these influence retirement migrants' experiences, and underscore the role that ageism plays in these insecurities. We briefly outline these dimensions in the following.

From national to international

Retirement migration within nation states in the Global North is a long-established phenomenon, with roots stretching back into the 18th and 19th centuries. In the UK, the creation of late-Victorian seaside towns provides one illustration (Kam, 1977; Warnes, 1993). Moving into the second half of the 20th century, a substantial increase in the scale of such migration was driven by greater prosperity among the baby-boom generation, along with changing attitudes about work and leisure in retirement (King et al, 2000; Gilleard and Higgs, 2005). In this context, while retirement migration was first an 'elite phenomenon' in the 1960s and 1970s, it 'acquired a broader social basis' and became more frequent over the last two decades of the century (King et al, 2000: 89).

International retirement migration covers a large range of practices and contexts. Some retirees are first-time migrants, while others migrated at a young age and return to their home countries later in life. Some are part-time migrants, while others live permanently in their host countries (King et al, 2000; Torres, 2012).[3] Retirement migrants can also move across national borders temporarily or permanently, with tourist visas or as official residents, and they may travel back and forth between two or more countries. Finally, although some migrants relocate after reaching full retirement age, others are early retirees. Among the latter are those who voluntarily retired and applied for retirement benefits in advance of full eligibility; others have been forced to stop working sooner than they had wanted and before reaching full eligibility.

The diversity in the geographic, temporal and administrative features of retirement migration makes it complicated to evaluate its magnitude (King et al, 1998, 2000; Pickering et al, 2019; Sloane and Silbersack, 2020). Yet, existing data help us to capture the significant quantitative changes that this phenomenon has undertaken over the last 30 years. For instance, in 2000, King and colleagues (2000: 25) showed that between 1994 and 1997, the number of British pensioners living abroad increased by 7.3 percentage points. In Spain, the number of immigrants aged 65 years old and over increased from 5.2 per cent in 1990 to 15.1 per cent in 2015 (UN, 2016). Sloane and Silbersack (2020) highlight that a similar trend is visible in the US, where 413,428 US Social Security (SS) beneficiaries received their cheques overseas in 2017, while in 1999, this figure was 219,504.

Precarity, later life and ageism

The concept of precarity is used to depict the increasing risks and insecurities of having insufficient resources for overcoming diverse obstacles (Dannefer and Huang, 2017; Grenier et al, 2021). Key to the notion of precarity is that despite the focus of neoliberalism on personal responsibility for household poverty, these risks are not under the control of individuals (Grenier et al, 2017). Thus, as we use it here, precarity involves both such structural aspects as welfare state retrenchment in a context of globalisation, neoliberalism and labour market instability, and the experience of anxiety that these provoke (Lain et al, 2019; Fine, 2021; Grenier et al, 2021; Phillipson, 2021).

Recent scholarly contributions to the study of later-life precarity include the work of Lain et al (2019, 2021), Grenier et al (2021), Phillipson (2021) and Simmonds (2021). Such research has shown how economic and social uncertainty increasingly shapes older people's lives in the countries of the Global North. The peculiarity of this observation lies in the fact that these countries developed policies during the 20th century aimed at securing later-life living conditions, particularly those related to retirement and health insurance. These policies were meant to provide the security that would allow older people to participate in society as fully as ever without having to worry about the future (see Chapter 3). Yet, despite such provisions, a significant portion of the older population faces economic and social insecurities, as we discuss further in this book.

Scholars of ageing have recently argued that 'extending the analysis of precarity to the later years naturally moves into questions of "what it means to be human" and to live a "devalued life" in a variety of contexts' (Grenier et al, 2021: 4). Frailty is one such context, which we view in light of the politics of healthcare, 'in relation to the construction of devalued subjects' (Grenier et al, 2021: 9). Implicit in this reference to devaluation is *ageism*: the denigration of old people because of their age. In this book, then, we take up the call to view later life in terms of precarity, while also showing that ageism is itself a source of much of the precarity of later life.

Age relations and ageism

Although scholars generally accept the reality of ageism, the basis, shape and consequences of this form of discrimination are rarely explored systematically beyond the pioneering work of Butler (1975). Harkening to similar inequalities, such as those based on gender or race, Butler pointed to ageism as involving not just attitudes but exclusionary behaviour. Indeed, a fair amount of more recent research finds that stereotypes and prejudices are not always correlated with behaviours; having a negative (or positive) view of older people need not translate into any particular behaviour (de São José and Calasanti, 2023). As we conceptualise it, then, ageism refers to a situation in which those designated as 'old' are not just devalued but excluded from social life, including rights attendant to full adulthood (Calasanti, 2020).

Just as sexism is rooted in a system of gender relations, so too does ageism emerge from age relations – a system of inequality that privileges younger people at the expense of those who are older. Since ageism is embedded in social institutions, it need not be intentional and is often hard to see. Still, it is evident in, for instance, older people's loss of power and authority in relation to their bodies. Not only do doctors treat their complaints differently than those of younger people because of their age (see, for example, Olenski et al, 2020), but they can lose their ability to decide how they will be treated, and they can be drugged without their consent. Further, older workers are marginalised in the labour market and often pushed out of employment; finding re-employment in comparable jobs is often nearly impossible (Roscigno et al, 2007; Lassus et al, 2015; Phillipson, 2019; Lain et al, 2021).

In conjunction with other inequalities, age categories become a convenient tool for questioning abilities and desirability in all realms of life (Bytheway, 1995). In the public sphere, older age is used to designate competence, a reality readily seen in US electoral politics, for example, wherein older candidates can be depicted as lacking the cognitive abilities needed to hold office. Whether intended or not, those of younger ages benefit from less competition for employment, positions of authority or intimate relationships (Calasanti, 2020). The devaluation of old people is perhaps most evident in the tremendous sway and profits garnered by the multibillion-dollar anti-ageing industry, which sells often dubious products and services to those trying to not be seen as old (Calasanti, 2016). Indeed, the ability of an industry to call itself 'anti-ageing' without protest from consumers attests to people's anticipation of a loss of status and exclusion, and their willingness to try to forestall their social demotion (Calasanti and King, 2017).

As we use it in this book, then, age is a social category that, depending on context, can designate someone as 'old' and thus at risk of devaluation and exclusion. Our discussion of precarity in later life thus examines both aspects: the ways in which this can emerge over the life course (Grenier et al, 2021); and the ways in which ageism itself impacts precarity.

Economic aspects

Welfare state policies significantly shape both the form and extent of precarity in later life (Lain et al, 2019, 2021). For instance, over the last 40 years, austerity plans and neoliberal policies in many welfare states of the Global North have decreased people's ability to foresee a secure future (Grenier et al, 2021; Phillipson, 2021). An illustration is the interaction between increased risks of facing long-term unemployment later in working lives and the postponement of full-retirement age in many countries, leading to a growing income gap between the age of the end of work and the age of eligibility for retirement pension (Lain et al, 2021; Repetti and Phillipson, 2020). Their financial situation allows some older people a choice as to when they will retire, according to their preferences; however, others face constraints that leave them few options for securing a livelihood for themselves and their families before and after retirement age (Grenier et al, 2021; Lain et al, 2019, 2021). Additional social transformations affecting households, such as divorce or family restructuring, can mean that some older people with lower incomes also face prolonged responsibilities for dependent family members (adult children, children and grandchildren) (Lain et al, 2021). In such contexts, attempts to maintain employment and income can be thwarted by job instability, ageism in the labour market or dead-end, low-paid jobs. Therefore, while some people continue to work beyond retirement age, this does not necessarily portend economic security.

Ageism in the labour market influences older workers' ability to maintain employment well before the age of retirement (Macnicol, 2006, 2015). Research shows that age-based discrimination can affect middle-aged workers, who can face long-term unemployment and occupy precarious jobs. For instance, in Switzerland, the US and the UK, unemployed workers over 50 years old are more likely than younger ones to face long-term unemployment (Lain, 2012; Lassus et al, 2015; Repetti and Phillipson, 2020). Further, ageism intersects with other systems of inequality, such as gender and class, to shape older workers' discrimination in the labour market. As a result, women and working-class members are especially likely to face precarious employment, a situation that threatens their ability to earn a living (Lain et al, 2019, 2021). It can also impact their access to healthcare; in the US, for example, people under the age of 65 are covered by healthcare insurance through their employers, and if not, they must pay for it out of pocket (Dickman et al, 2017). Insecure ends of work lives can also affect people's abilities to contribute to retirement plans, to save money or to collect good, earnings-based pensions, all of which negatively impact their resources after retirement (Lain et al, 2019, 2021; Repetti and Phillipson, 2020).

Social aspects

Scholars emphasise that precarity in later life can include social aspects, by which we mean the risk of being excluded from communities based on social status, independently from economics. In such contexts, people lack the ability to participate in key domains of social life (Grenier et al, 2021; Lain et al, 2019, 2021; Phillipson, 2021; Warburton et al, 2013). Lain et al (2019, 2021) also emphasise the ontological consequences of precarity, namely, anxiety regarding the ability to anticipate future economic and social needs, particularly when faced with risks in relation to such areas as work, the welfare state and family.

However, scholars typically do not focus on the ways in which social precarity articulates with ageism in later life independently of class. Yet, ageism induces social precarity because it creates a risk of social exclusion for older people independent of their economic resources (de São José and Calasanti, 2023). In this book, we address this gap by looking at the social precarity produced by ageism, which we define as the risk of social exclusion because of advancing age. We will show that this form of social precarity can be key in understanding the experience of retirement migration.

Health aspects

Precarity in later life can manifest in relation to health, not from illness or injury per se, however, but from the context in which needs for medical care arise. This context is shaped, first, by welfare state policies on healthcare, often in interaction with (generally female) family members' availability. When healthcare policies are insufficient and when families cannot provide such care, older people may struggle to find good-quality and affordable care, which can contribute to the production of health-related precarity (Hall, 2021; Simmonds, 2021). This can lead them to relocate to where the cost of healthcare is lower, such as to a different country. However, such strategies may not resolve the precarity that older people face, for instance, migrants may face language barriers or lack of knowledge about the healthcare systems in different countries (Hall, 2021).

To this, we include a second consideration: ageism may also add to health-related precarity, regardless of welfare state policies, family availability or wealth. Age relations influence the construction of health, such that the illnesses and injuries that occur in later life are perceived differently than those of younger people. This can result in different therapeutic interventions and treatments, such as psychotherapy for younger people versus drugs for those who are older (Robb et al, 2002). Age-based variations in diagnoses and treatment have important impacts.

Daily assistance

More incremental changes in abilities can also be a part of ageing, such that old people come to need assistance in daily life. Such help can range widely; it can include such intermittent tasks as cooking and cleaning, also known as instrumental activities for daily living (IADLs) (Guo and Sapra, 2020), which allow one to function and maintain independent community living; and it can involve tasks associated with personal care, such as eating or bathing, often referred to as activities of daily living (ADLs) (Katz et al, 1970).

As with incontinence or poor mobility, need for assistance can increase at any point in the life course; however, it is approached differently based on age (Fine, 2021). This disparate treatment impacts everything from medical treatment to assistance and, again, state policies (Wyman et al, 2018). Long-term support for infants and young children demands significant investment from families and the state. Yet, because they are more highly valued, children are typically not perceived as burdens due to their care needs, whereas older adults are. Therefore, when such assistance concerns younger groups and children, they are not perceived as a problem, whereas older people are (Calasanti, 2020).

For the most part, welfare state policies do not provide this assistance on a continuing basis; as a result, the loss of abilities in later life presents an additional form of precarity (Hall, 2021). Most assistance must be obtained informally, typically from family members or peers, or formally through paid care. Lacking family members or others who are willing and able to provide help, or having insufficient funds to pay for such care, threatens older people's ability to maintain some level of personhood. In some situations, people may hire migrant care providers or relocate abroad where they can afford cheap care (see, for example, Bender et al, 2017; Repetti and Schilliger, 2021). However, the latter can also fall short of securing an older person's life, as Hall (2021) showed in relation to British retirement migrants in Spain. We will examine this form of precarity in Chapter 7.

Book structure

The book begins with a review of the literature on international retirement migration and precarity in later life in Chapter 2. It first presents the different aspects of these geographic movements since the 1980s, particularly in relation to lifestyle transformations in the Global North, welfare state developments and reforms, family relations, and local and global power relations. The chapter also discusses the links between retirement migration, precarity in later life and age-based discrimination. We then present the context of the study, our participants' nationalities (British, Swiss and US Americans), their demographic profiles, the three countries where the fieldwork was conducted (Spain, Costa Rica and Mexico) and the different periods of time during which it took place (mostly between 2016 and 2020). We also provide a brief description of our methodology, which involved semi-structured interviews.

Chapter 3 outlines interactions between precarity and the welfare state in our participants' three home and host countries. We focus on health and pension policies in the UK, Switzerland and the US. We compare the similarities and differences between these policies in how they cover the population and how they shape different forms of precarity in later life. Additionally, we highlight these policies' origins in liberal ideologies and the implicit assumption that individuals are responsible for foreseeing their future and overcoming their insecurities in later life, while the state's support is complementary. We end the chapter by describing retirement migrants' access to pensions and healthcare in the three host countries.

The next three chapters present our findings in relation to forms of precarity. In Chapter 4, we show how retirement migration can be a response to economic precarity. We begin by discussing the differences and similarities in our interviewees' experiences of migration, including regarding the life stage at which they migrated, that is, before or after reaching formal retirement age. In addition, we look at the costs of living that retirement migrants consider as having a significant impact on their situations in their home and host countries, and how these vary according to national welfare states in the UK, Switzerland and the US. Finally, we emphasise the economic precarity that can remain in retirement migration contexts, including the difficulty of anticipating the future.

Chapter 5 addresses the linkages between retirement migration and the social precarity resulting from ageism. First, we describe the ageism that results from age relations, in which people lose value with age, become excluded and are faced with a denial of their full adulthood. We then show that in their host countries, retirement migrants feel that they are treated with respect and valued, rather than seen to be a burden or dependent. They have opportunities to contribute to the local economy and community in ways perceived as supportive to the community. In addition, they generally live among other retirement migrants, which helps them feel accepted and included. They contrast their treatment with that in their home countries, where they find that older people are marginalised. Finally, we show that for female participants, retiring abroad can be a way to escape from gender-based discrimination and to gain more freedom.

Chapter 6 focuses on the global privileges that allow retirement migrants to deal with different forms of precarity. First, we show that transnationalism – namely, the ability to travel across frontiers easily and regularly – draws on global privileges linked to retirement migrants' national citizenship. In addition, we discuss migrants' access to a relatively cheap global market of communication and travel, which allows them to maintain family and social ties, as well as access to healthcare, in their home countries. Second, we show that our interviewees' social positions can be both precarious and privileged, depending on local and global intersecting inequalities. We observe that their sense of inclusion in a host country draws on exploitative social and economic interactions with the local population and environment, and that these relations also shape retirement migrants' views of the local population. Finally, we address retirement migrants' idealisation of local people's attitudes and behaviours towards older people, which they believe to be composed of spontaneous affection and deference for them as older people. In particular, they view women in the host countries as being natural, loving and inexpensive caregivers, a depiction that plays an important role in their strategising for assistance in later life and addressing the precarity resulting from the loss of abilities. We highlight the ways in which global inequalities and postcolonialism shape the opportunities that retirement migration represents, as well as the social status of retirement migrants and their interactions with the local population.

Chapter 7 addresses precarity linked to health and assistance in later life. We discuss the links between age relations and the social construction of health. The lower value attached to older people's lives compared to those of younger people influences how healthcare practitioners approach them and the kinds of treatments they receive. We also point to the increased need for support in daily activities that can accompany declining abilities, as well as the challenges that this poses for people with inadequate means to address these needs. We show that retirement migration can be a way for people to try to deal with such healthcare and assistance precarity. Abroad, they can find care that they describe as both cheaper and 'loving', a context shaped by the cheap workforce composed of local women.

Our conclusion returns to the aim of this study and presents a summary of how it contributes to work on retirement migration. We highlight our main findings concerning the diverse forms of precarity (economic, social, health and assistance) that shape retirement migration, how those interact with global and local systems of inequalities, and the reality that retirement migration is only a temporary solution. We also point to the role of welfare states, labour markets and households in shaping retirees' decisions to relocate and their migration experiences. In particular, we discuss the ways in which age relations factor into the retirement migration experience, from the more obvious role in labour markets and welfare state policies, to ageism and healthcare and assistance needs. In looking towards future research and policy, we suggest that the demarcation between the international migration of younger and older people based on economics versus family reunification or leisure obscures the economic situations and contributions of older people in the context of globalisation. We urge scholars and policy makers to rethink the ways in which older migrants are perceived and to recognise the continuing precarity that old age brings regardless of economic position.

2

Retirement migration

Introduction

Scholarship over the last 40 years has explored the contexts in which retirement migration unfolds, how these have changed over time and the diversity in retirement migrants' motivations and experiences. We depict increasing precarity as a social fact resulting from neoliberalism and austerity trends in the Global North (Phillipson, 2021), one that results in anxiety about the future (Lain et al, 2019, 2021; Grenier et al, 2021). To some extent, such precarity has been related to ageism, whether in terms of discrimination in the labour market or welfare state policies (see Phillipson, 2021). Often overlooked, however, is that ageism (and the specific impacts it has on precarity) also influences older people's plans and experiences, including those of international retirement migration. In this chapter, we discuss the importance of examining how ageism influences precarity and the experiences of retirement migrants. We point to global inequalities borne of colonialism, wherein accumulation was centred in countries of the Global North, many of which occupied, dominated and exploited the people and natural resources of countries in the Global South. In the present era of unequal global relations, the 'unequal accrual of privileges and rewards from a global system of production and accumulation' (Hayes, 2018a: 11) undergird retirement migrants' statuses and options, as well as shape their interactions with local populations. We end the chapter with a description of our study, which took place in Spain, Costa Rica and Mexico, and of our sample, which was composed of Swiss, British and US retirement migrants.

Retirement migration: what do we know?

Retirement migration has drawn attention from scholars in North America since the early 1980s, as it has become a more frequent practice (Calzada and Gavanas, 2018). Some early studies focused on seasonal migration to the US Sunbelt – that is, the movement of North American retirees (US and Canadian citizens) to the warmer regions of the US for the winter. Longino and Biggar (1981) conducted some of the first research on seasonal and permanent North American retirement migrants' social ties and interactions in the US Sunbelt. They showed that the retirees who migrated permanently to these areas fostered the integration of those who came only for a couple of months every year and that, together, the two groups constructed communities. Other studies of seasonal North American migrants in the Sunbelt have shown how class, race and age shaped where they chose to relocate, as well as their housing and their quality of life in the new location (Sullivan and Stevens, 1982). These previous scholars did not use the concept of 'precarity', which only emerged in the social sciences in the 1990s and even later in social gerontology (Grenier and Phillipson, 2018). Yet, they identified linkages between uneven economic and/or social resources and retirement migration in later life. Since these first studies in the 1980s, international retirement migration has been the subject of a growing literature about retirees' relocation to other areas of the world, especially Central and South America (see, for example, Longino and Marshall, 1990; Sunil et al, 2007; Bantnam-Masum, 2015; Hayes, 2015).

In England, King and colleagues (1998, 2000) developed the first major studies in the mid-1990s. Their work focused on British retirees who relocated to Southern Europe, particularly to Spain, which was, and still is, a favourite destination for British retirement migrants. King and colleagues shed light on the motivations for British citizens to retire abroad, finding that they were mostly privileged people wanting to adopt a lifestyle that better suited their cultural identities, reflecting their social status and social capital. As in the US, as such relocation has grown, social scientists have studied the retirement migration trend among British citizens, focusing not only on Spain but also on other locations, especially in Southern Europe and Asia (see, for example, O'Reilly, 2007; Phillipson, 2007; Oliver, 2008; Benson and O'Reilly, 2009; Ahmed, 2015).

In Switzerland, research on this phenomenon emerged at the turn of the 21st century. Spain is also a favourite destination for Swiss retirees, and following the work of King and colleagues, early Swiss studies analysed both the motives of older Swiss people and the strategies that they developed to create a sense of security, home and belonging abroad (Huber, 1999a, 1999b, 2003a, 2003b; Huber and O'Reilly, 2004). In addition to Spain, more recent research has focused on such destinations as Morocco and Thailand, and has explored Swiss retirement migrants' social and material security abroad, as well as their transnational family relations (see, for example, Bender et al, 2017, 2018; Bender and Schweppe, 2022; Repetti et al, 2018; Repetti and Bolzman, 2020; Calasanti and Repetti, 2018; Repetti and Schilliger, 2021; Bolzman et al, 2022; Schweppe, 2022a).

As the number of international retirement migrants has continued to rise, so too has the literature exploring the experiences of retirement migrants living in regions around the globe, mostly in Central and Southern America, Southern and Eastern Europe, and in Southern Asia (see, for example, Teh, 2018; Sloane and Silbersack, 2020; Sone and Thang, 2020; Schweppe,

2022a). These studies cover such topics as migrants' search for a particular lifestyle, the wish to travel regularly as well as to move back, and the changes in, and maintenance of, family ties. This research has also illuminated the role played by global power relations in retirement migrants' relocation possibilities and their experiences in the host country. We then develop linkages between retirement migration, precarity and ageism.

Lifestyle factors

Several early studies of retirement migration present the decision to relocate as driven by a generation of relatively privileged retirees hoping for travel and other leisure. For instance, King and colleagues (1998, 2000) depict such retirees as having enough good health and money to allow them to choose a new, sunny location for their later years. This situation is based upon diverse factors. First, increased life expectancy and better health in later life mean that some retirees change how they think about their futures. With more years of active life expectancy, they can consider ways to enjoy a different, more carefree life. Second, thanks to post-Second World War prosperity and the expansion of retirement pensions in Europe during the second half of the 20th century, older people's material conditions have improved. In addition, national policies facilitating access to housing among the middle class in the second half of the century allowed this generation of retirees to purchase homes that they could then resell at a profit when they retired (King et al, 1998, 2000).

The rise in popularity of retirement migration was also driven by the development of a mass tourism industry from the 1980s, with housing and leisure markets aimed at attracting people of richer countries to come to cheaper areas of the world (Rainer, 2019). Adding to this was the increased availability of cheap means of communication (phones and, later, the Internet) and transportation (for example, lower-cost flights) from the 1990s onwards, trends that accelerated in the 21st century (O'Reilly, 2000; Gustavson, 2008; Oliver, 2008; Benson and O'Reilly, 2009; Benson, 2011; Hall and Hardill, 2016).

In a more nuanced analysis of retirees' choices, Phillipson (2007) argued that the impacts of globalisation on labour and communities have helped to reshape neighbourhoods in countries of the Global North. Together with the dismantling of traditional family and local community ties, the gentrification of neighbourhoods, especially in urban areas, put new constraints on older people who aged in place. They could end up living in a neighbourhood with which they no longer identify and in which their social ties have weakened. However, in other contexts, globalisation has provided retirees with a large range of choices regarding the kind of lifestyle that they 'elect' (Phillipson, 2007: 330) to pursue in later life. Rather than being relegated to ageing in a place that is no longer familiar, some older people find migration to present an opportunity to reside in a new location that reflects their lifestyles and pasts, and to thus reconfirm their identities (Phillipson, 2007: 329). Along similar lines, Gambold (2013: 193) found that for single women, retiring abroad could furnish a way to have a stronger sense of freedom regarding how they want to live in retirement, as well as a way to 'reinvent themselves' through choices that they would not have been able to make in their home country (see also Hayes, 2018a). Other retirement migration scholars underscore retirees' cultural motivations for choosing their new area, such as loving specific natural and architectural surroundings or particular weather, or wanting to discover different cultures (Sunil et al, 2007; Benson and O'Reilly 2009; Hayes, 2018a; King et al, 2019, 2021). In such contexts, Phillipson (2007: 330) argued, migration can reflect older people's choices and dynamic identities.

Adding to this cultural framework, retirement migration can result from a process of individualism typical of the post-Second World War generation, shaped by the destruction of traditional institutions and a sense of social obligations. According to this view, retirees of this generation no longer see themselves as linked to their community and families, and in relocating abroad, they seek to engage in the kind of life that they want, regardless of social expectations (Ahmed, 2015). Along these lines, retirement migration results from retirees' will to engage in 'active' and 'successful ageing' (Hayes, 2018a), models of ageing promoted in countries of the Global North that are meant to challenge the negative depiction of older people (Katz, 2000; Katz and Calasanti, 2015; Timonen, 2016; Repetti, 2018). Yet, as we discuss in Chapter 5, this argument does not take into account why people want to engage in such normative models of ageing. That is to say, it ignores the ways in which ageism shapes the choices that people make, including the quest to not fit ageist stereotypes of older people.

Ease of travel

Some research has focused on the importance of geographic movement in international retirement migrants' experiences, that is, the ability to travel regularly between their host and home countries. Some retirees engage in seasonal migration, keeping two homes in two different areas of the world, while others relocate permanently. However, in both contexts, the ease of travel is a critical dimension of retirement migrants' experiences (King et al, 2000; Cohen et al, 2015; Lardiès-Bosque et al, 2016).

International retirement migrants do not just relocate and construct new lives in a new country; they often maintain a transnational social life and make sure that returning home remains an option. In this context, the ability to travel is critical to migration and to maintaining relations in the home country, especially with family, and, in some instances, accessing healthcare for complex medical procedures and treatment. The distance between host and home countries (where retirees' families most often live), as well as existing travel infrastructure and costs, are often important considerations when retirees choose a destination. In addition to car or train travel, living close to airports with frequent flights can become particularly critical when retirees' families need support, or when retirees need to return quickly or frequently to their home state for health or bureaucratic reasons. Retirement migrants also need to have sufficient economic resources to afford such travel and, sometimes, to pay for lodging while in the home country. Conversely, the inability to be geographically mobile can create risks of losing ties with families and friends, and of being unable to provide and receive the level of care and support that retirees or their families may need. In sum, avoiding the risk of becoming stuck in the host country is often key to international retirement migrants' security (King et al, 2000; Hall and Hardill, 2016; Lardiès-Bosque et al, 2016; Gehring, 2017; Pickering et al, 2019; Repetti and Calasanti, 2020; Repetti and Lawrence, 2021).

Finally, retirees regularly traverse national borders, which means that they rely on international agreements that regulate the global movement of people (Hall and Hardill, 2016; Gehring, 2017). Health and economic conditions after migration also depend on international agreements concerning migrants' ability to access welfare state provisions abroad and to travel between countries (Acker and Dwyer, 2004; Longino and Bradley, 2006; Ma and Chow, 2006; Hall and Hardill, 2016; Lardiès-Bosque et al, 2016; Botterill, 2017; Gehring, 2017; Repetti and Bolzman, 2020). For instance, in Europe, being a member of the European Union (EU) or an associated state facilitates movement between countries. As these international relations change over time, they offer more opportunities or pose more constraints to retirement migrants (see Chapter 3).

Transnational family ties

Retirement migrants have diverse relationships with their families. Some have weak family ties, and relocating abroad does not significantly change them (see, for example, Schweppe, 2022b). However, for retirement migrants whose family ties are strong, moving to a new country can present greater challenges for maintaining those relationships, particularly when family members were used to spending a significant amount of time together. Some scholars argue that retirement migrants desire to disengage from family relations and obligations by relocating abroad (Oliver, 2008; Ahmed, 2015; Woodspring, 2016). Previous work provides some nuance to this view, pointing to the significant role that family can continue to play in retirement migrants' experiences and the latter's desire to maintain ties. Even while living abroad, many retirees travel in order to provide care and support to their families, either in cases of emergency or through regular and planned visits. They also regularly host their families, either for vacation or when family members need support. For instance, grandparents often take care of their grandchildren during summer or holiday breaks and on vacation (Repetti and Calasanti, 2020; see also Repetti and Lawrence, 2021). In addition, retirement migrants and their families are likely to maintain relations by using such communication technologies as the telephone, video chats, messaging, email and other online networks (such as Facebook) (Ahmed, 2015; Repetti and Calasanti, 2020).

Living abroad without family nearby can also become challenging for retirement migrants. Some miss their kin, even if they maintain family relations transnationally and develop strong social networks in their new location (Ahmed, 2015). This situation can become even more difficult when they face unexpected events involving emotional, social or physical changes, such as the loss of loved ones or the development of health problems. In addition, although some retirees may have resources sufficient to afford private care or be entitled to access public healthcare in the host country, the family-based organisation of informal care in the host country can present issues to those whose families live far away (Hall and Hardill, 2016; Oliver, 2017). Thus, it is important for retirement migrants to be able to return easily to their home country (whether temporarily or permanently) (Sone and Thang, 2020; Repetti and Lawrence, 2021).

Retirement migration and global relations

Increasingly, scholars point to a global structure of inequalities that provides retirement migrants with economic and social privileges in their host countries. They show that relations between the retirees' home and host countries often reproduce postcolonialism, especially when retirees relocate to former colonies. In these countries, retirement migrants can benefit from cheap labour, cheap access to land and a valued status, all of them rooted in social structures inherited from colonialism. These structures continue to shape economic, political and social relations today, both within these countries and between them and the Global North (Bell, 2017; Benson, 2015; Rainer, 2019; Hayes, 2018a, 2021). This global context provides retirement migrants with privileged statuses in their new locations, while portending less clear-cut impacts on local economies and social cohesion in the host countries. On the one hand, retirement migrants often provide local workers with more job opportunities in sectors like domestic labour, real estate and retail. On the other hand, they also use their 'geopolitical privilege' (Ciafone, 2017: 160; see also Hayes, 2018a) to take advantage of cheaper workforces and land. A retirement migrant community can contribute to an 'amenity property boom' (Rainer, 2019: 40), adding to a process of gentrification in poorer countries. The resulting increased cost of living and housing makes residing there less affordable for local populations, a situation about which they complain (Rainer, 2019) and about which retirement migrants are either unaware or unconcerned because they see it as normal (Hayes, 2018a, 2018b; Miles, 2015). Second, retirement migrants tend to socialise primarily with each other, forming communities bounded by formal or informal relations, but engaging infrequently with the local people, thereby reinforcing the boundaries between retirement migrants and the local population, instead of facilitating interactions between the two groups (Benson, 2013, 2015; Hayes, 2018a, 2018b, 2021).

Such global relations are especially visible in both healthcare provision and policies for assistance with ADLs. For instance, some US early retirement migrants who are not yet eligible for health insurance (see Chapter 3) describe themselves as 'healthcare refugees' (Miles, 2015: 43), as healthcare in the US is too expensive for them. In their host country, they rely on the cheaper medical costs and local workforce. Along similar lines, Gavanas (2017) shows that Swedish retirement migrants in Spain hire low-cost local workers for occasional daily healthcare and assistance with daily activities. This global market of healthcare and assistance – which is part of the 'global care chain', that is, the 'series of personal links between people across the globe based on the paid and unpaid work of caring' (Hochschild, 2014: 250) – can be a critical factor underpinning retirees' decision to relocate. Thanks to their 'relative privilege' (Benson, 2015: 21) of coming from the Global North, migrating to the South can allow these retirees to access such inexpensive formal and informal healthcare and assistance (see, for example, Bender et al, 2018; Hayes, 2018a, 2018b, 2021; Rainer, 2019).

Thus, retirement migration reflects the global system of inequalities from which those in the Global North benefit. Owing to this, retirement migration is available not only to wealthy retirees but also to members of the middle class (Hayes, 2018a). Retirement migrants can use their relative global privileges to choose to relocate abroad and live a new 'adventure' (Hayes, 2018a: 46) in a poorer country. They can also access cheaper healthcare, an important benefit when they cannot afford such care in their home countries. However, more recently, researchers have also underscored the role that precarity, and not just wealth, plays in retirees' motivations to relocate from richer countries to those where the costs of living are lower.

Retirement migration and precarity

Motivations for retirement migration can be rooted in global privilege, but they can also reflect the impact of neoliberal and austerity welfare policies related to ageing in richer countries (Phillipson, 2021). Relocating to a poorer country can be a response to the subsequent precarity experienced by older people in these richer countries, as they contemplate how to deal with limited incomes (Gambold, 2013; Hayes, 2018a).

Based on these considerations, and following preliminary studies (see, for example, Hardill et al, 2005; Oliver, 2008; Benson and O'Reilly, 2009), recent research has explored the ways in which both precarity and privilege interplay in retirement migration contexts (see, for example, Botterill, 2017; Ciafone, 2017; Oliver, 2017; Bender et al, 2018; Hall, 2021). Although they may well be advantaged by their social status in their host countries, social inequalities also differentiate among retirement migrants as a group (Botterill, 2017). For instance, scholars have highlighted inequities between those retirement migrants who are economically privileged and those for whom migration is a way to escape from precarity (Bantnam-Masum, 2015; Bell, 2017; Botterill, 2017; Repetti et al, 2018; Hayes, 2021). Research on both Mexico and Ecuador has revealed gender differences, such that women, especially those who are single, see their migration as a way to cope with low incomes (Gambold, 2013; Hayes, 2018a). Although retirement migration can be undertaken to secure their economic position, retirement migrants can experience precarity in the host country as well, where they risk losing the economic and social advantages that they gained by relocating abroad (Repetti et al, 2018). Such emergent precarity can result from changes in financial or health situations in the household (for example, widowhood), or in global political contexts (for example, alterations in transnational agreements concerning pensions) (Botterill, 2017: 5). Changes in geopolitical relations, such as the 2016 referendum which determined that the UK would leave the EU ('Brexit'), or economic instability at the national and international levels can have critical consequences for retirement migrants' ability to anticipate their economic security in the host country. Those persons whose financial situation has remained tenuous in their new location are especially vulnerable in this regard (Repetti et al, 2018; Brook and Jackson, 2020).

Hayes (2018a) found that retirement migrants' desires to maintain good health motivated their relocation, as they felt that engaging in an active or successful ageing lifestyle was possible only if they lived abroad. Access to good-quality medical treatment is also critical and tied to different welfare state policies. Some seek cheaper healthcare, as did some from the US who may not have coverage otherwise (Hayes, 2018a); others, such as those from the UK, sought access to their home country's healthcare coverage in their new location. Retirement migrants often face new and complex healthcare needs in their new countries at some point, and research makes clear that finding good care can be challenging for a number of reasons (see, for example, Hardill et al, 2005; Hall and Hardill, 2016; Botterill, 2017; Oliver, 2017; Hall, 2021). First, retirement migrants' inability to import specific public health plans (such as financial support for long-term care) from their home state into their host country, as well as the absence thereof in the host country, can prompt precarity (Hall, 2021). Some may opt to pay for private health insurance if they can afford it, but others may have no health insurance at all and face dire consequences. Along these lines, Botterill (2017) shows that low-income British retirement migrants in Thailand find affording healthcare to be quite difficult, as they lack free access to healthcare in the country, and as private hospitals are expensive, their ability to receive medical treatment is constrained, at best.

Second, long-term care or assistance with daily living are particular concerns. In Spain, Hall (2021) finds that British retirement migrants are faced with a lack of publicly financed care assistance, resulting from the Spanish policy assumption that families will provide such aid. For those who cannot afford private care, the growing health or assistance needs that can emerge with advancing age become major sources of precarity. Even when economic resources are not a problem, a lack of mastery of the local language and of understanding of the healthcare system can make it difficult for retirement migrants to find the care that they need (Hall, 2021). The need for healthcare or help with ADLs and IADLs can be especially challenging for heterosexual women, as their longer life expectancies mean that they are less likely than men to rely on a partner for care, if they have one. They thus need to develop strategies to secure access to care (Gambold, 2013). At the same time, research suggest that long-term care needs can cause female retirement migrants to return to their home country after the loss of a partner (Botterill, 2017). For their part, heterosexual men are more likely to have a partner – either one who relocated with them or one whom they met in the new location – to whom they can turn for care (Botterill, 2017; Bender et al, 2018; Repetti and Bolzman, 2020).

Retirement migrants' legal status in the host country often requires such conditions of residence as annual fees and visa renewals, and some migrants do not meet these mandates. As a result, they can be caught in a situation where they are without full citizenship in either their home or host countries, and have no economic or political rights, as well as no pension, in either place (Botterill, 2017). Retirement migrants may also struggle to develop new social links with other migrants or the local community, to speak the local language, and/or to understand the ways in which public and private administrative services, healthcare systems, or private businesses work in their new countries. Thus, even though retirees might gain more security by relocating abroad, migration can also simply postpone (or generate) risks, such as the danger of becoming caught in the host country with low economic, legal and social resources (Hall and Hardill, 2016; Botterill, 2017; Schweppe, 2022b).

In sum, the migration of some retirees from the Global North to poorer countries facilitates a more secure economic situation in later life and better access to healthcare, housing, food and leisure. For others, however, the situation in the new country remains – or becomes – precarious, a result of unstable pensions, healthcare costs that are too high or inability to move back home (Hall and Hardill, 2016; Botterill, 2017; Oliver, 2017; Rishworth and Elliott, 2019; Schweppe, 2022b). Precarity, as well as strategies to deal with different dimensions, are thus dynamic, and outcomes are not guaranteed.

Retirement migration and ageism

Ageism represents another basis for precarity that can influence retirement migrants' decisions and experiences. Although scholars generally accept the reality of ageism, the basis, shape and consequences of this discrimination are rarely explored systematically beyond the pioneering work of Butler (1975). Harkening to similar inequalities, such as those based on gender or race, Butler pointed to ageism as involving not just attitudes but exclusionary behaviour. Indeed, a fair amount of more recent research finds that stereotypes and prejudices are not always correlated with behaviours; having a negative (or positive) view of older people need not translate into any particular behaviour (de São José and Calasanti, 2023). As we conceptualise it, then, ageism refers to a situation in which those designated as 'old' are not just devalued but excluded from social life, including rights attendant to full adulthood (Calasanti, 2020).

Just as sexism is rooted in a system of gender relations, so too does ageism emerge from age relations, a system of inequality that privileges younger people at the expense of those who are older. Since ageism is embedded in social institutions, it also need not be intentional and is often hard to see. Still, it is evident in older people's loss of power and authority in relation to their bodies. Not only do doctors treat their complaints differently than those of younger people because of their age (see, for example, Olenski et al, 2020), but they can also lose their ability to decide how they will be treated, and they can be drugged without their consent. Further, older workers are marginalised in the labour market and often pushed out of employment; finding re-employment in comparable jobs is often nearly impossible (Roscigno et al, 2007; Lassus et al, 2015; Phillipson, 2019; Lain et al, 2019, 2021).

In conjunction with other inequalities, age categories become a convenient tool for questioning abilities and desirability in all realms of life. In the public sphere, older age is used to designate incompetence, a stigma readily seen in US electoral politics, for example, wherein older candidates can be said to lack the cognitive abilities needed to hold office. Whether intended or not, those of younger ages benefit from any reduction in competition for employment, positions of authority or intimate relationships (Calasanti, 2020). The devaluation of old people is perhaps most evident in the sway and profits garnered by the multibillion-dollar anti-ageing industry, which sells often dubious products and services to those trying to not be seen as old (Calasanti, 2016). Indeed, the ability of an industry to call itself 'anti-ageing' without protest from consumers attests to people's anticipation of a loss of status and exclusion, and their willingness to try to forestall their social demotion (Calasanti and King, 2017).

Ageism and the equation of old age with dependence leads many people in the Global North to view older people as burdens on their families and the larger society. Thus, the political treatment of older people assumes or conveys that old age is a problem for social cohesion. For instance, policy makers and entrepreneurs can depict old people as a hindrance in the labour market when they continue employment past a certain age. They are viewed as problems: as taking jobs away from younger workers and not making room for the next generation; as obsolete; or as obstructing advances that could enhance productivity. At the same time, and regardless of the accuracy of the claims, policy makers often depict the retired population as a drain on the economy and nation because of pension costs borne by states and companies (Estes and Phillipson, 2002; Estes et al, 2003; Macnicol, 2015; Williamson and Beland, 2015; Repetti and Phillipson, 2020). Furthermore, most policy makers present the social protection of old people as a problem of personal, rather than social, risk management in old age (see Chapter 3). Likewise, healthcare experts call for older people to discipline themselves to 'age successfully' and avoid or delay reliance on others in their daily lives, including in relation to long-term care (Calasanti and King, 2021). Older people should remain active (Katz, 2000), even if this entails working in precarious jobs or in unpaid activities that can be physically demanding, such as engaging in care work for a partner or for grandchildren (Calasanti and Repetti, 2018). Finally, older people's contributions to their communities and the economy are undervalued, if recognised at all (Calasanti, 2006; Calasanti and Repetti, 2018; Repetti et al, 2022).

Ageism influences many aspects of older people's experiences. First, the high risk of long-term unemployment that older people face (Lassus et al, 2015; Phillipson, 2019) can have a tremendous impact on their security in later years. Not only do they lose opportunities to invest in pensions or other savings for the future, but while they are without a job, they must also rely on any money they have set aside to see them through. Health problems can be particularly challenging in this context of economic insecurity. Insufficient economic resources in later life can also prevent the intergenerational transfers that often occurred in the past and that younger generations facing precarity increasingly need (Lain et al, 2019; Repetti and Phillipson, 2020). Second, ageism shapes old people's social inclusion and sense of belonging in these countries. The systematic devaluation that they confront by virtue of looking or being older, the reduced opportunities for them to take part in social activities, and the lack of recognition of their contributions to families and communities results in marginalisation and, sometimes, social isolation (Calasanti, 2006; Gibbons, 2016). Third, while all older people face ageism, its onset, intensity and consequences vary according to status in other intersecting systems of inequality. For instance, in many countries, women are likely to be seen to be old at younger ages than are men, and given life-course inequalities based on gender, they are more likely to face material deprivation. At the same time, older men who are minority group members may experience greater financial insecurity than more privileged older women (Calasanti and Slevin, 2006; Calasanti, 2020).

Retirement migration studies rarely address ageism, though some authors refer to it as an aspect of retirement migration trends (see, for example, Ciafone, 2017; McHugh, 2000). To be sure, scholars have discussed the advantages that retirees gain by relocating abroad, and some authors analyse these in relation to the disadvantages that old people can face in their home countries in the Global North. Some also address the role that states play in pushing citizens to find individual-level solutions to the precarity that they face in later life. However, to date, none of this literature addresses ageism as a system of inequality situated at the core of the political treatment of old people. Yet, this inequality can be key to understanding retirement migrants' experiences regardless of their class and gender, their status as 'elected' or 'excluded' (Phillipson, 2007: 321), and their social positioning.

Our study

This book draws on semi-structured interviews conducted with early retirees and retirees living permanently in Spain, Costa Rica and Mexico. As we spent time in these communities, we also draw on our less formal conversations and experiences in these locations. Although we interviewed people coming from diverse European and North American countries, we focus on a subsample ($N = 79$) composed of British ($N = 14$) and Swiss ($N = 12$) participants located in Spain, as well as US participants living in Costa Rica ($N = 25$) and in Mexico ($N = 28$). We interviewed them all in person between 2016 and 2020. In addition, 15 were re-interviewed in 2021 and 2022; the aim of this second round was to explore possible changes in participants' lives. The COVID-19 pandemic hit just after we finished our fieldwork in early 2020; only the re-interviews occurred after that time. As the bulk of our analysis is based upon the initial data collected, the book does not address the effect of the pandemic on retirement migrants' lives.

We conducted the interviews in English with the British and US participants, and in French or German with the Swiss participants, translating the latter into English for analysis. The first author conducted the interviews in Spain and Costa Rica, and the second author conducted those in Mexico. They took place in the towns where participants spent time, either at their home or in cafes; the second set of interviews were conducted remotely via Skype, Zoom and similar applications, or by telephone. Most interviews were conducted one on one, though on rare occasions, couples did not want to be interviewed separately. To preserve anonymity, we changed all participants' names and we do not provide detailed information about where they lived, in either their home or host countries. We also use pseudonyms for the locations where the interviewees lived.

At the time of the first interviews, the participants' ages ranged from 52 to 83 years old, with a mean age of 66. A total of 47 participants were women and 32 were men; 61 lived with partners and 18 lived alone. All had lived in their new country for more than a year (see Table 2.1).

The fieldwork took place in one city and two towns in Spain, three towns in Costa Rica, and one small town and surrounding area in Mexico. All were located by oceans, with the exception of one area next to a lake. These towns appear to be typical of retirement migration locations. In Mexico, one of our respondents maintained that two thirds of the community were 'expats'. While he was likely referring to a small geographical area, that a large number of retirement migrants lived in these areas was apparent in their presence in cafes, streets and shops. In addition, the local companies, infrastructures and services were clearly developed for North – South migrants, particularly retirees, rather than for locals, with a high number of bars, medical services and international food stores. The towns also presented significant differences. The city in Spain contained more than 400,000 inhabitants. Study participants lived downtown or in suburbs. The other participants in Spain lived in two small towns of around 25,000 inhabitants in the same seaside region. Some participants lived in downtown areas, while others lived in neighbourhoods at enough distance from the downtown

Table 2.1: Demographic profile of the interviewees

	All	Men	Women
All	79	32	47
Mean age	66	66	66
Single	18	5	13
Partnered	61	27	34
British	14	3	11
Swiss	12	6	6
US	53	24	29

centre that they needed a car to manage daily life (for example, to go to the supermarket, to the pharmacy, to cafes and so on). The infrastructure in all three Spanish areas was in good shape and allowed for ease of movement, whether by car, public transportation or walking, as well as easy access to shopping centres and healthcare services. From Switzerland and the UK, it was possible to reach these places easily by airplane, boat, train or car.

These Spanish locations contrasted with the three areas studied in Costa Rica. All were situated in very rural and remote areas, several hundred kilometres away from the capital, where most of the supermarkets and healthcare facilities were located. Travelling between the capital and these towns was possible only by car and took many hours, requiring driving on small, twisting roads across mountains and through rainforests. Some roads were paved, but most were not, and in case of heavy rain, roads were often impassable. The locations where the interviews took place were small villages with 2,000 or fewer inhabitants.

The majority of respondents in Mexico resided in a town of under 1,000 people, while the rest lived in the surrounding area, within about 20 kilometres. Retirement migrants seemed to dominate the area in terms of numbers, though locals lived there as well. One could walk to a small grocery or cafe if needed, but the town was located close enough to a larger city of about 70,000 (and another, even larger but more distant, city) to enable one to drive there if one needed more goods and services than were offered locally. Located by the sea, as well as on a well-travelled, paved road, neighbourhoods were mostly gated, though depending on their location, these were sometimes more symbolic than functional, as they only closed off direct road access.

Although the local language in all the studied areas was Spanish, many businesses, stores and services used English, and some used German or French. It was also apparent that retirement migrants and local people did not mix as much as they could, as our interviewees' neighbourhoods were predominantly inhabited only by North – South migrants. Migrants and the local populations mostly interacted in retail locations.

Conclusion

Retirement migration is not a new phenomenon. However, over the last 40 years, it has accelerated, and many scholars depict it in terms of upper- and middle-class retirees who wish to age successfully and actively, and search for new adventures. Postcolonialism shapes their opportunities, giving them privileged economic and social statuses in their host countries. Along these lines, retirement migration can be seen to be a continuation of exploitative relations between richer and poorer nations in the Global North and South.

Recent scholarship reveals that such migration can also be a strategy to overcome economic precarity in later life, with uneven success. Retirement migrants can gain more financial security, though uncontrolled events can also disrupt their plans. While such tactics are developed at the individual level, they do so in a context where governments in the Global North seek to 'outsourc[e]' older people (Gambold, 2013: 194; see also Ciafone, 2017) or 'offshore retirement' (Hayes, 2018a: 35) in order to reduce public expenditures (Croucher, 2022). This tactic reflects ageist assumptions that older people are a burden and the expectation that older individuals (and their families), rather than the state, are responsible for addressing their needs.

In this book, we examine the relationship between retirement migration and different dimensions of precarity. As we will show, one aspect of precarity is economic and concerns people who withdraw from the labour market in later life, either before or after retirement age. This group faces financial insecurities with negative consequences for their abilities to afford such needs as housing, food and health; relocating abroad can be a way to overcome such risks. We also discuss social precarity, which relates to the loss of status that people experience when they grow older and that they may try to avoid by relocating abroad. We also address health-related precarity, which entails the risk of being unable to access healthcare, as well as receiving different or lower-quality treatment based on age. Finally, we explore the precarity that results from the inability to obtain the needed assistance to deal with loss of abilities and maintain daily life and autonomy. This situation emerges when older people lack family support or provisions from the welfare state. As we will show in this book, all these forms of precarity can be linked to ageism and can encourage people to relocate in a new country in later life.

3

Precarity and the welfare state in home and host countries

Introduction

Retirement migration is not only about geographical movement but also about people navigating between the policies of different states, such as those related to old age, public health insurance and residence or citizenship requirements. In countries of the Global North like the UK, Switzerland and the US, older people often rely on welfare state benefits for their economic security and their access to healthcare. In this context, the economic and health benefits that retirement migrants receive from their home countries, as well as whether they can access their state pensions and local healthcare systems in their host countries, influence their decisions about whether and where to migrate.

In this chapter, we use literature on work, retirement and health policies in later life to explore the political-economic contexts shaping the precarity of older people in the UK, Switzerland and the US. These three countries present especially interesting cases for study. On the one hand, they all contain retirement regimes and healthcare policies which assume that individuals (and their families) have the primary responsibility for security in later life. On the other hand, they provide different levels of protection to older people, both in terms of old age and retirement benefits, and ability to access healthcare.

In the following, we present an overview of the welfare state policies for later life in the three countries and indicate how they shape precarity at retirement age. We also discuss retirement migrants' access to pensions and healthcare in their host countries: Spain, Costa Rica and Mexico.

Welfare state policies for later life in the United Kingdom, Switzerland and the United States

Retirement and health policies are key to the ageing experiences of people in the countries of the Global North (Estes and Wallace, 2010). In terms of the former, since the Great Depression in the US and the Second World War in Switzerland and the UK, authorities have enacted policies aimed at reducing poverty among older people at the national level. As we will show, healthcare policies across these nations are rather varied. The British National Health Service Act (adopted in 1946) provides free healthcare to all, regardless of age. In the US, Medicare (adopted in 1965) offers low-cost access to basic healthcare to people aged 65 and over. Switzerland has no public healthcare scheme specific to older people. However, the Health Insurance Act (adopted in 1996) mandates that all residents purchase a healthcare plan from a private insurance company.

Several scholars (for example, Béland, 2002; Leimgruber, 2008; Rogne et al, 2009; Williamson and Béland, 2015; Repetti and Phillipson, 2020) have shown that these public policies reflect liberal ideals, that is, the belief that individuals, families and private organisations have primary responsibility for providing economic security and access to care in later life. In this regard, the state is meant not to replace the roles of persons and the market in securing later life but to complement these efforts instead. Further, these policies are rooted in capitalist structures, wherein each pension benefit is linked to income earned during each person's life course, a calculation that reproduces inequalities in the labour market, such as those based on gender. As a result, after retirement, women (and especially minority racial and ethnic women) in these countries are more likely to face poverty than are their male counterparts, which reduces their ability to afford goods and services, including healthcare (Sullivan and Meschede, 2016; Calasanti, 2020).

In what follows, we describe pension and health policies in the UK, Switzerland and the US. We compare these three countries to each other and to other European and North American nations. Despite the differences among the three countries, we find that the gaps in policy coverage are such that many older people still face precarity. We also outline how these welfare states vary, producing or reproducing both similar and different kinds and levels of deprivation in later life.

United Kingdom

Pension policies

In the UK, the national pension (the basic state pension), implemented in 1946, comprises a universal contribution-based first pillar (Fraser, 2003; Walker and Foster, 2006; Williamson and Béland, 2015). It is financed through workers' and employers' contributions, and provides small pensions, lower than the costs of living. Benefit levels are tied not to growth in average earnings but to inflation (Bozio et al, 2010). Older adults are meant to supplement these with other sources of income, such as personal occupational and private pension plans. None of these plans ensure a certain level of benefits in retirement; that amount depends on the insured person's ability to manage their financial investments and savings (Walker and Foster, 2006; Williamson and Béland, 2015). Since the 1960s, the UK government has provided a universal state pension and encouraged workers to contribute to an occupational plan. During the Thatcher premiership in the early 1980s, several reforms increased the role of private savings within the British old age insurance regime, strengthening the responsibility of individuals, rather than the state, in securing old age (Williamson and Béland, 2015). Austerity policies have decreased the proportion of the national income spent per pensioner in the UK since the 1980s (Bozio et al, 2010: 67) and increased the number of people continuing to work after retirement age (Lain et al, 2019, 2021; see also OECD, 2022). Finally, the British retirement scheme includes a means-tested supplementary plan (the British Pension Credit) aimed at providing financial support to older people with income below the poverty line (Gov.UK, 2022). Of note for our study, the British basic state pension, as well as other private pension plans, can be collected while living abroad.

The way in which these policies shape retirees' financial situations and their likelihood of poverty can be seen in Table 3.1. These numbers point to the percentage of income derived from state or state-regulated programmes. They also show the percentage of the older population faced with poverty in these countries. These figures make clear that although state retirement policies and programmes are meant to provide older people with some level of economic security, a significant minority are still left with income insufficient to meet basic needs. According to the Organisation for Economic Co-operation and Development (OECD, 2022),[1] in 2018, 42.8 per cent of older people's income in the UK was derived from the basic state pension and other public transfers, such as means-tested benefits. Although this percentage is similar to what we find in Switzerland and the US, it is significantly lower compared to other neighbouring countries, where an average of two thirds of retirees' incomes are derived from these state sources. Even with means-tested benefits, 15.5 per cent of people aged 66 and older in the UK were poor in 2018, compared to 12.4 per cent in the whole population. Further, the poverty rate varies by gender: in 2018, 18 per cent of women and 12.6 per cent of men in the UK were poor. Still, as we discuss later, this percentage is lower than it is in Switzerland and the US.[2]

Finally, to decrease public expenditures, in 2007, the UK government raised the state pension eligibility age for women from 60 to 65 years old (Bozio et al, 2010). Since then, the full retirement age for men and women has been equalised to age 66, and the UK government plans to raise the retirement age to 68 for both groups by 2039 (Gov.UK, 2017).

Health policies

In the UK, older people are covered by universal medical insurance through the National Health Service (NHS). Introduced in 1946, the NHS covers basic medical care services financed through income taxes; prescription drugs, as well as dental, vision and hearing care, are free of charge for people aged

Table 3.1: Income sources of older people and poverty rate

	UK	Switzerland	USA	14 neighbouring countries[a]
Income sources after 65 years old				
Public transfers	42.80%	42.50%	41.30%	66.30%
Occupational transfers	30.10%	29.19%	7.60%	6.47%[b]
Capital (including saving and assets)	11.70%	14.10%	15.90%	11.30%
Work	15.30%	14.30%	35.30%	15.94%
Poverty rate				
Total population (after taxes and transfers)	12.40%	9.20%	18.80%	9.44%
After 66 years old (after taxes and transfers)	15.50%	16.50%	23.10%	7.94%
Men (before taxes and transfers)	12.60%	14.70%	19.60%	6.14%
Women (before taxes and transfers)	18.00%	18.00%	25.90%	9.38%

Notes: [a] Austria, Belgium, Canada, Denmark, Finland, France, Germany, Ireland, Italy, Netherlands, Norway, Portugal, Spain and Sweden. [b] Only Denmark, Germany, the Netherlands and Sweden have occupational plans.
Source: OECD (2022).

60 and over (Roll, 2009). When we began our study, NHS benefits could be collected in other European countries. However, since the UK left the EU in 2021, this is no longer possible. According to the OECD (2022), in 2019, 100 per cent of the population in the UK was covered by the NHS and 78.5 per cent of people's healthcare costs were paid by the UK government. The other 21.5 per cent of the costs were covered by individuals (including co-payments, private complementary insurance premiums and other out-of-pocket costs). Still, personal contributions to care costs have increased over the last decade.

British legislation makes a distinction between 'healthcare', which is covered by the NHS, and 'social care', which is not. Healthcare includes 'all forms of healthcare provided for individuals, whether relating to physical or mental health, and also includes procedures that are similar to forms of medical or surgical care', while social care is 'personal care and other practical assistance provided for individuals who by reason of age, illness, disability, pregnancy, childbirth, dependence on alcohol or drugs, or any other similar circumstances, are in need of such care or other assistance' (Article 9 of the Health and Social Care Act 2008[3]). As a result of this distinction, individuals must often pay for most of the costs of care that are not considered strictly medical (Simmonds, 2021). Older people with long-term medical care needs can apply for extra funds for in-home medical care (NHS, 2022). Some of those who cannot afford social care rely on their family, particularly women of all ages, who are the ones most likely to perform most social care (Simmonds, 2021). Others whose family cannot provide this must rely on public means-tested financial support and charitable organisations to pay for this care (NHS, 2021; Simmonds, 2021).

In sum, the British pension and health regime provides older people with a basic, universal contribution-based state pension. About a third of older people's income is derived from occupation-based plans, but nobody can count on a particular benefit level for their retirement. The entire system is contribution based and reproduces the income inequalities that exist at earlier stages of the life course, including those between men and women. The NHS covers the whole population and the state finances more than three quarters of people's healthcare costs. However, most non-medical care – which is provided predominantly by women – is not covered, a situation that is especially problematic for older people needing assistance with daily life. This latter group must pay for most of this care out of pocket or receive unpaid support from their families and charities.

Switzerland

Pension policies

In Switzerland, the Old Age and Survivors' Insurance Act (hereafter, basic old age insurance) was introduced by the Confederation[4] in 1947. Full retirement age for men is 65; women's age was originally 65 but has changed over time and presently stands at 64 (see Repetti, 2018: 152–3). The insurance is contribution based, and it is compulsory for everyone; those who do not work for pay contribute to a minimal contribution. Benefits are indexed to the wage and inflation rate. Similar to the UK (and the US, as we will see), this insurance is not sufficient to meet the cost of living, and people need other sources of income in later life. Contributions constitute 80 per cent of the programme's financing, with complementary support (20 per cent) from the federal state.[5] For those who hold jobs, the 80 per cent contributions are split 50–50 between employers and employees. Poorer older people can receive supplementary benefits based on a means test (History of Social Security in Switzerland, 2020). In addition, since 1985, the basic old age insurance is complemented with two other schemes. This system, known as the 'three-pillar pension regime', includes a compulsory occupational pension plan and a tax benefit for individuals who contribute to private pension plans. Workers earning more than a certain yearly income[6] must pay into an occupation retirement plan, to which employers must also contribute. In contrast to the UK (and the US, as we will show), employees' and employers' minimal contributions and benefit levels are dictated legally by the Confederation; the latter income depends upon the earnings of the insured. In addition, people can put money into a tax-free individual savings plan from which they cannot collect before retirement age (History of Social Security in Switzerland, 2020). However, both the occupational and savings plans can be collected before reaching retirement age for those individuals who relocate abroad. Those living in other countries can also receive their basic old age insurance there.

Turning to the impact of these policies and again looking at Table 3.1, we see that according to the OECD (2022), in 2018, 100 per cent of the population was covered by old age insurance. In addition, and similar to the UK, 42.5 per cent of older people's income came from the basic old age insurance and other public transfers. Also like in the UK, the inequalities that structure the labour market are reproduced after retirement age. Further, in 2018, 16.5 per cent of people aged 66 were poor – somewhat higher than in the UK but lower than in the US – and this proportion was higher for women (18 per cent) than for men (14.7 per cent). This percentage is particularly elevated compared to the whole population (9.2 per cent), making Switzerland the country with the highest level of age-based inequalities in poverty risks of our three studied countries.

As with the UK, the last 30 years have seen federal authorities try to raise the age threshold for full eligibility and reduce benefit levels for both the basic old age insurance and the occupational pension plan. They presented their actions under the guise of controlling increased public costs due to the ageing of the population and to respond to a perceived need for austerity measures in public spending (Leimgruber, 2013). Between 1997 and 2002, women's full eligibility for the basic old age insurance and the occupational pension plan increased from age 62 to 64; in 2022, a proposal to increase women's full retirement age to 65 in 2024 was accepted by Parliament (Federal Social Insurance Office, 2023). Other implemented reforms have modified the occupational benefit plan, including a reduction in the benefit level of pensions (Federal Social Insurance Office, 2016).

Health policies

It was only in 1994 that a mandatory, universal basic health insurance policy was implemented in Switzerland through the Health Insurance Act (LAMal), which covers people regardless of their age. The insurance is provided by private companies and requires monthly premiums and beneficiaries' co-payments. The federal health insurance pays for a large range of acute and long-term medical provisions based on a list that the Confederation sets out; however, costs related to vision, hearing, dental health and wellness programmes are not covered. The costs of the monthly premiums vary according to the chosen insurance carrier (even though all insurance policies cover the same list of health costs). Based on free-market economic assumptions and on the claim that healthcare beneficiaries are clients able to choose their insurance according to their best economic interests, the law allows people to change insurance companies once each year. When people have insufficient incomes, cantons supplement people's contributions to the insurance. For those who are poor, these cantonal subsidies cover all individual financial contributions to health insurance and healthcare costs, including co-payments (History of Social Security in Switzerland, 2020). The insurance does not cover Swiss people living abroad.

According to the OECD (2022), 100 per cent of the population in Switzerland is covered by federal health insurance. The Swiss state and the federal health insurance pay for about 64 per cent of people's healthcare costs, and the rest is paid by individuals through federal health insurance premiums and co-payments, private complementary insurance premiums, and out of pocket. The cost of healthcare treatment is high compared to the UK (OECD, 2022), which means that healthcare can consume a significant part of individuals' and families' budgets. In addition, as with the UK, federal health insurance covers only those costs considered to be medical; additional assistance with personal care or daily life generally must be paid for privately, that is, out of pocket or through private insurance. In this context, older people must often rely upon their families for assistance, the responsibility for which is likely to fall primarily on women, or, if affordable, on the private care market (Anchisi and Despland, 2010; Schilliger, 2015; Schwiter et al, 2018). Thus, receiving the care or assistance they need is often a critical issue for older Swiss people, particularly those who have limited means (Dallera et al, 2014, 2015).

To conclude, the Swiss retirement and health regime presents both similarities and differences with the British system. Both countries provide a basic, universal pension benefit based on old age insurance, as well as universal health insurance. Coverage from the latter insurance is limited to those healthcare provisions considered medical and does not include other forms of support, such as that for ADLs, typically needed in long-term care contexts, or IADLs. Differently from the UK, however, the Swiss programme includes compulsory occupational insurance for people earning a certain income; further, the minimum level of employers' and employees' contributions and of the benefit amount is specified by the Confederation. Another variation between these countries lies in the individual's role in the financing of healthcare, which is significantly higher in Switzerland than in the UK. Particularly costly are individuals' contributions to the basic healthcare insurance (premiums and co-payments), as well as the financing of private complementary insurance and the provisions paid out of pocket. The fact that medical treatment is particularly expensive in Switzerland adds to the burden of healthcare costs for Swiss people, particularly in later life.

Differences and similarities in retirement and health insurances in the UK and in Switzerland influence the experiences of ageing in these countries and the challenges that people face as they age in finding income security and access to healthcare. In the US, described in the following, we see that retirement policies are also linked to earnings in ways that are likely to reproduce inequalities in later life. At the same time, healthcare access in later life differs from the British system, a universal, free programme that is not age based, and the Swiss insurance system, which is also not age based, though is government regulated and requires relatively high premiums paid to private insurers. As we will see, the US system conforms to neither: citizens are covered by a government-run healthcare programme only when they have reached age 65, and for which they must pay a basic premium to receive medical coverage beyond basic hospitalisation costs. Despite the variations across these countries, gaps in income security or healthcare access, or both, can result in precarity in later life.

United States

Pension policies

In the US, the Social Security Act 1935 provided a contribution-based pension. In contrast to the Swiss and British basic old age insurances, SS is not universal but covers people who participate in the labour market for a minimum number of quarters and their dependants. Further, only workers and employers contribute to the SS fund, not the federal government. Since 1973, SS benefits are indexed to the inflation rate (Rogne et al, 2009). Similar to the British Pension Credit and the Swiss supplementary old age benefits, the US also has the Supplemental Security Income (SSI) programme, a means-tested assistance benefit for older people whose incomes are well below the poverty line. In contrast to the Swiss system, though similar to the UK, the US does not have a compulsory, occupation-based pension policy (Williamson and Béland, 2015). Employers decide whether to offer occupational pensions; most are defined contribution plans (such as 401ks), wherein eventual benefits are not predetermined but instead depend on how much money is invested and how well these funds have done in the market. Further, contributions by employers and employees alike are typically optional. People who contribute to some of these pensions (for example, 401k) or to individual retirement savings accounts (IRAs) are not taxed on that income at the time of contribution. However, these types of retirement accounts are not equally available to all workers. Contributions assume a level of disposable income generally not available to members of the working class and many women, and require financial acumen or advisors (Williamson and Béland, 2015). Both SS and private retirement pensions can be received while living abroad.

Turning again to the data in Table 3.1, we see that in 2018, the income sources in later life in the US reflect both similarities and differences with the British and Swiss contexts. As with the other two countries, the level of income provided by the state is relatively low (41.3 per cent). However, the proportion covered by occupational transfers (7.6 per cent) is much lower than for the UK and Switzerland. This is accounted for by a major difference in income sources across these three countries: one third of older people's income (35.3 per cent) in the US comes from paid work, a particularly high proportion compared to the two other countries, as well as to other neighbouring countries (see Table 3.1). The poverty rate among people aged 66 and older is also much higher in the US (23.1 per cent), reflecting but going beyond the relatively high poverty rate for the whole population (18.8 per cent). As we saw with the British and Swiss contexts, gender also shapes the risk of poverty in the US, with one in five men (19.6 per cent) and one in four women (25.9 per cent) living in poverty. In all three countries, then, we see a sizeable minority of older people living in poverty or at risk of poverty, with women particularly likely to be in financial straits.

Finally, older people's sources of income in these three countries are less reliant on government transfers than is the case in other European nations (see Table 3.1). Yet, we see that, just as has happened in the UK and Switzerland, the 1980s have seen members of the US government seeking to reduce public expenditures, arguing that the free-market economy would respond to people's needs better than the state (Estes, 2004; Rogne et al, 2009; Estes and Wallace, 2010; Williamson and Béland, 2015). Policy makers maintained that old people are dependent upon the state and are thus a problem for societal well-being (Calasanti, 2020). Reflecting these trends, legislation passed in 1983 mandated a slow increase in the full retirement age from 65 to 67 by 2027.

Health policies

No universal health insurance coverage exists in the US, though the Affordable Care Act 2010 mandated that most people be covered by health insurance, either through their employer or through the healthcare marketplace (comprised of private insurance companies) (see Table 3.2). Those workers who do have health insurance through their employers lose it when they become unemployed or retire.[7] Health insurance purchased through the marketplace can be quite expensive and is thus most accessible to those with economic privilege. However, since 1965, Medicare, a basic hospitalisation and medical insurance policy for people over 65 years old (Medicare.gov, no date), covers those eligible for SS.[8]

The contemporary Medicare programme is composed of four parts. Traditional Medicare includes Parts A and B. Part A, financed by payroll taxes, is hospitalisation insurance that, after a deductible, covers: inpatient hospital stays (within certain limits); short-term, post-hospital skilled nursing facility care after a three-day hospital stay; limited home healthcare; and hospice care. Part B provides supplemental medical insurance and covers doctors and outpatient care, medical supplies, some home healthcare, and some preventative services. To be covered by Part B, recipients must pay a monthly premium, as well as co-payments; the remainder is paid by the government. Traditional Medicare does not cover prescription drugs, vision, hearing and selected other services. To make up for this gap in coverage, some Medicare beneficiaries have supplemental insurance; however, most do not have this coverage (Federal Interagency Forum on Aging-Related Statistics, 2020: 122). Additionally, about one quarter of older people opt for Part C ('Medicare Advantage'), an alternative to traditional Medicare. Part C is a 'managed care plan' provided by private organisations, generally including a group of doctors, hospitals and other healthcare providers, which agree to provide care to Medicare beneficiaries in exchange for a fixed amount of money from Medicare every month. Typically, these managed care plans include services not covered by traditional Medicare, including eye exams, and prescription drugs; they also require that members use only their doctors and services. However, Part C is not available in many areas. Finally, in 2006, legislation established Part D – paid through individual premiums, co-payments and government contributions – which includes optional prescription drug coverage through private insurance carriers (Medicare.gov, no date). However, Part D can be expensive (for both the premiums and co-payments), and plans can drop drugs, increase their costs and so on when desired.[9] Lengthier home healthcare, personal care and instrumental assistance are not covered by any form of Medicare; institutional long-term care may be covered by Medicaid, a means-tested programme for those who are poor. Medicare does not cover healthcare needs for US people living abroad.

In addition to Medicare, Medicaid was created by the federal government in 1965 to provide access to healthcare, prescription drugs and long-term care to people with low incomes of all ages and for people with disability in the US (Medicaid.gov, no date). Thus, older people who are poor can receive institutional, custodial care (at facilities that accept this form of payment) through this programme, as well as help with prescription drug costs. However, many kinds of healthcare, such as that related to vision and hearing, and assistance with daily living outside of an institution are not covered by this or any US programme.

In 2018, according to the OECD (2022), 34 per cent of the US population was covered by a government-paid health plan, including Medicare; however, when we look at those aged 65 and over, almost 100 per cent of that population were covered by Medicare (Robin et al, 2021). Yet, similar to Switzerland, the monthly premiums and cost-sharing requirements of Medicare means that individuals' contributions to healthcare expenses are still quite high. Out-of-pocket healthcare costs represent as much as 19 per cent of disposable income for poor and low-income elders, a proportion that increases to 26 per cent among those over age 85 (Federal Interagency Forum on Aging-Related Statistics, 2020: 51). In addition, healthcare in the US is expensive compared to the UK and other neighbouring countries, even slightly more than in Switzerland. This increases co-payments and can represent a major economic burden for individuals, especially for those with low incomes.

In conclusion, and similar to the British and the Swiss systems, being financially secure in later life in the US requires that people have income sources beyond SS. As a result, inequalities among older people are higher than among other age groups (Crystal et al, 2016); this is further illustrated by poverty rates by gender, race and ethnicity (Calasanti, 2020). In addition, healthcare coverage in the US is limited. Medicare does ensure healthcare financing for older people, but this coverage is partial and often inadequate because, as in Switzerland, people must pay a significant amount for premiums and cost sharing. In all three countries, the provision of both assistance and long-term care is inadequate, which means that people with such needs and reduced income are likely to rely on family or charity in a significant way.

Retirement and health policies in a context of neoliberalism

As observed in the previous section, the British, Swiss and US retirement and health policies present similarities as well as differences in their historical changes and their current provisions. First, after a period of an increased state role in securing later life from the 1930s and 1940s, the 1980s witnessed the beginning of neoliberal policy makers' push to privatise old age risks, rather than address them in collective terms (Estes and Phillipson, 2002). They have also raised the age of access to retirement pensions or full benefits, as previously discussed. This neoliberal thrust continues to shape people's ability to plan for and experience a secure later life today (Grenier et al, 2020, 2021; Phillipson, 2021). These three countries are similar in that policy makers place the primary responsibility for later-life security onto individuals (and their families) and the market for mitigating the risk of poverty and healthcare needs. Reflecting this trend, the states play a relatively limited role in securing retirees' income, compared to neighbouring countries (see Table 3.1). Furthermore, the three national pension regimes tied benefit amounts to labour market earnings over the life course (see Table 3.2). In addition, in Switzerland and in the US, health insurance costs are high, a situation that further reduces financial security in later life.

At the same time, we can see differences among the UK, Switzerland and the US retirement and healthcare policies. Only the Swiss system contains a mandatory occupational pension with legally defined contributions for employees and employers, as well as defined benefits. The UK government has strongly encouraged workers to contribute to such a pension, and retirement pension plans cover a significant part of British retirees' income. However, the UK government does not ensure a level of protection for these retirement plans, and the benefits depend more on insured people's financial strategies and the market. In the US, occupational pensions comprise a particularly small part of later-life income compared to Switzerland and the UK. The high level of poverty in later life in the US (see Table 3.1), reflects the particularly liberal and privatised nature of the US retirement scheme. As some scholars have observed (for example, Williamson and Béland, 2015; Calasanti, 2020; Simmonds, 2021), since the levels of economic protection afforded by retirement pensions are inextricably linked to beneficiaries' work lives, these policies are likely to reproduce inequalities in later life based on such social statuses as gender and class. For instance, the gender gap in labour market pay results in women being more likely to face economic deprivation in later life than men. As shown in Table 3.1, this phenomenon is especially visible in the US, though gendered poverty rates are also prevalent among the British and Swiss.

In all three countries, the financial wherewithal to pay for private health plans or out-of-pocket costs plays a major role in older people's ability to obtain healthcare, particularly among those with long-term care or daily assistance needs. The cost of healthcare itself further influences older people's ability to avail themselves of it. In the US, the high cost of healthcare increases out-of-pocket costs. The impacts of similarly expensive healthcare in Switzerland are somewhat cushioned by the compulsory healthcare system, such that affording healthcare is more feasible for older people than in the US, but it can still represent an issue. In the UK, annual per capita healthcare costs are relatively low (USD 4,521), with significant coverage from the government. Given this, affording healthcare is generally less challenging than in the two other countries. However, in all cases, affording personal care and instrumental help can be difficult, as those involve help like domestic work, forms of assistance not covered by governments or compulsory healthcare schemes in any of the three countries.

Table 3.2: Differences and similarities in retirement and healthcare policies in the UK, Switzerland and the US (2020)

Kind of policy	UK	Switzerland	US
Social insurance for income security	Basic state pension since 1946 – Universal coverage – Full benefits begin at age 66 – Full benefits start after 30 years of paid contributions – Depending on individuals' earnings	Old age insurance since 1946 – Universal coverage – Full benefits begin at age 64 (women, rising to 65 in 2024) and 65 (men)	SS since 1935 – Covers workers and dependent spouses – Full benefits begin at age 66, rising to age 67 by 2027
Occupational benefit plan for income security	Optional defined contribution plans	Compulsory occupational benefit plan since 1982 for workers with a yearly income of CHF 21,330 and over	Optional defined contribution plans
Social assistance for income security	National assistance since 1948 – Complements or replaces state pension – On a means-tested basis Replaced by supplementary benefits in 1966 Replaced by income support in 1988 Replaced by the minimum income guarantee in 2003 Replaced by Pension Credit in 2003	Supplementary benefits since 1964 – Complements state pension – On a means-tested basis	SSI since 1972 – Complements or replaces state pension – On a means-tested basis
Social insurance for access to healthcare	NHS since 1946 – For all ages – Financed through income taxes – Covers some medical care, but drug prescriptions and dental and eye care are partially charged – Free of charge for people 60 and over – Residential care not covered	LAMal since 1994 – For all ages – Financed through premiums and contributions; public subsidies for poorer people – Covers a range of acute and long-term medical care and prescription drugs – Vision, hearing, dental and wellness care not covered – Long-term non-medical care not covered	Medicare since 1965 – For people aged 65 and older – Part A free of charge for those entitled to SS; basic hospitalisation insurance (and short-term rehabilitation); financed through payroll taxes – Parts B is medical insurance, financed through monthly premiums, individual contributions and (mostly) government

Table 3.2: Differences and similarities in retirement and healthcare policies in the UK, Switzerland and the US (2020) (continued)

Kind of policy	UK	Switzerland	US
Social assistance for access to healthcare	Attendance Allowance since 1971 – Covers long-term care needs for people over state pension age – Basic financial support for day and night care providers – On a means-tested basis	Supplementary benefits since 1964 – Covers basic healthcare provisions paid by the LAMal – On a means-tested basis	– Part C is financed through monthly premiums; covers A, B and D as well as hearing, vision. – Part D is prescription drug insurance, financed through premiums, co-payments and (mostly) government – No long-term care coverage Medicaid since 1965 – Covers institutional long-term care – On a means-tested basis

The implementation of healthcare and old age policies has had positive effects on financial security and access to care among older people in all three countries, and they are still considered to be especially successful anti-poverty policies (Haber and Gratton, 1993; Phillipson, 1998; Rogne et al, 2009; Repetti, 2018). However, although these policies continue to be important, as we have seen, a significant portion of older people still experience precarity today, shaped by a lack of economic security and limited public financial support for healthcare or assistance with daily life. Thus, older people in all three countries can face these different forms of precarity, and these can, in turn, shape retirement migration experiences. As we discuss in the coming chapters, retirement migration is tied to the retirement and healthcare policies of sending countries and can thus be an answer to the economic, health and support risks that some older people face in their home nations. In the next section, we explore retirement migrants' access to pensions and healthcare policies in receiving countries, as these also shape the political-economic context of this international movement.

Retirement migrants' access to pensions and healthcare abroad

Given the data on poverty after retirement, especially in the US (see Table 3.1), some continue to work well beyond their retirement age in order to gain financial security (Swain et al, 2020). Still others relocate to different regions or entirely new countries to obtain better access to healthcare and improve their economic security. Reflecting this, some scholars depict retirement migration as a way for countries to 'outsource' (Ciafone, 2017: 155) older people by encouraging them to move to poorer countries, thereby ridding richer countries of portions of their populations for whom they do not want to provide. From this vantage, retirees' decisions to migrate can be seen to result from the incapacity of neoliberal welfare states to ensure a decent old age for all of their citizens (Gambold, 2013; Gavanas, 2017; Ciafone, 2017).

In addition, retirement migrants' living conditions are shaped by the economic inequalities between the home and host countries, the welfare state policies accessible in destination countries (see Table 3.3), and international agreements (Sloane and Silbersack, 2020). For Swiss, British and US retirees, inexpensive options to access retirement benefits and healthcare provisions exist in such countries as Spain, Costa Rica and Mexico. In principle, accessing policies from one's home country is especially easy in Europe, thanks to the international agreements within members of the EU. Although Switzerland is not a member state, the Swiss government has specific agreements with the EU that facilitate their citizens' access to governmental policies abroad (Eur-Lex, 2004). Swiss retirees can thus receive their monthly retirement pensions in Spain without having to pay

Table 3.3: Swiss, UK and US retirement migrants' access to welfare state policies in Spain, Costa Rica and Mexico

	Spain	Costa Rica	Mexico
Access to home state pension	Swiss and British retirees can receive a pension from their home country in Spain. It is without banking charge for the Swiss. For the British, it was free of charge until Brexit.	US citizens can receive their SS benefits via electronic transfer to a Costa Rican bank account with banking fees.	US citizens can receive their SS benefits via electronic transfer to a Mexican bank account with banking fees.
Access to state healthcare insurance	British and Swiss citizens who officially reside in Spain can access public healthcare insurance (Seguridad Social), which is cheap for people over 65 years old. Covers healthcare in Spain and in the UK, as well as in Switzerland under certain conditions. Income-based fee for drug prescriptions. Swiss citizens lose their access to Swiss healthcare insurance. British citizens keep their NHS coverage.	US retired citizens who officially reside in Costa Rica can access public healthcare insurance (Caja Costarricense de Seguro Social). Small income-based fee covers medical treatment and drugs provisions. US citizens can still use their Medicare insurance if they get treatment in the US.	US retired citizens who officially reside in Mexico can access public healthcare insurance (Seguro Popular). Small fee. Covers medical treatment and medicine provisions. US citizens can still use their Medicare insurance if they get treatment in the US.

Source: Convention de sécurité sociale entre la Confédération suisse et l'Espagne (1969), Eur-Lex (2004), Gov.UK (2019), Social Security Administration (2004), Sloane and Silbersack (2020), Rocío Sáenz and Acosta (2010) and International Living (2020).

banking fees. However, they must pay a basic monthly premium to be covered by the Spanish health insurance – the Spanish Seguridad Social (see Convention de sécurité sociale entre la Confédération suisse et l'Espagne, 1969: Article 17). When the UK was a member of the EU, British retirees could receive their pensions and access healthcare in Spain without banking fees. However, the UK's departure from the EU means the British retirees can no longer obtain pensions free of charge in Spain, and access to Spanish health insurance requires official residence in Spain and small fees (Gov.UK, 2019). US retirees can receive their SS benefits abroad with small banking fees (Social Security Administration, 2021). However, Medicare does not pay for healthcare outside the US (Sloane and Silbersack, 2020: 11). US retirees who have official residency in Mexico and Costa Rica can pay a basic amount of money to be covered by national healthcare insurances – the Caja Costarricense de Seguro Social or the Seguro Popular (Rocío Sáenz and Acosta, 2010; International Living, 2020; Sloane and Silbersack, 2020).

Still, lower costs of living and affordable healthcare are not the only factors important to retirement migration. Such movement can also reflect a wish to maintain or improve people's social inclusion. In this regard, economic precarity can matter, as sufficient financial resources can help to prevent marginalisation in later life (Grenier et al, 2020). However, older people risk social exclusion even when they have sufficient incomes, not only because of isolation or health issues (Grenier et al, 2020), but also due to ageism, which can impede older people's social participation (Calasanti, 2020). Wealth may forestall ageism, pushing its impact further into the future, but it does not eliminate it. Thus, retirement migration can be a way to avoid a form of precarity regardless of economic resources.

Conclusion

The UK, Switzerland and the US arrange their retirement and their health policies in similar as well as different ways. Old age insurance across these countries is organised around relatively small state pensions, based on policy makers' expectations that individuals should take responsibility for arranging the rest of their economic protection. In the UK and Switzerland, retirement policies also draw on the expectation that employees should contribute to an occupational pension plan; only in Switzerland, though, are such contributions mandatory for those who earn more than a certain yearly income, and contributions for employers and employees, as well as benefit levels, are legally specified by the Confederation. In the UK and the US, most of retirees' income is strongly tied to the capacities of the insured persons to manage their assets on the market, with consequent higher risks of losing money. In Switzerland, pension insurance companies invest their assets in the market, but the Confederation controls the pensions and is responsible for assuring that eligible people receive their pension benefits.

Overall, the old age insurance organisation in the three countries makes it possible for a large proportion of older people to receive minimal benefits and access to supplementary means-tested state support. However, it does not enable all older citizens to secure their material needs entirely, and we have seen that significant levels of poverty or near-poverty persist among older people in all three countries. To the extent that benefit levels are based on consistent labour market experience and higher wages, or provide opportunities and sufficient discretionary income to save for retirement through investing in pensions or tax-free savings, these old age insurance schemes tend to reproduce systems of inequalities based on such social statuses as class and gender. As a result, people's unequal labour market experiences are likely to be replicated in their later years.

In health policy, the British system differs from the other two by paying for a relatively large portion of the nation's healthcare costs. In Switzerland, federal healthcare insurance coverage is moderate, but healthcare is very expensive. As a result, healthcare expenditures are likely to weigh heavily on older people's budgets. In the US, the situation is different still: state coverage of healthcare costs is relatively low for the whole population, but Medicare covers almost all people aged 65 years and older. As in Switzerland, in the US, healthcare costs are very high, challenging older people's ability to access the healthcare they need. It can be especially problematic for US people who are not insured, such as those who have lost their employment benefits (through which they may have had healthcare coverage) prior to their eligibility for Medicare at 65 years old. This can also present significant challenges for older people, as they are more likely to face economic insecurities and have increased care needs, while Medicare only covers a limited portion of healthcare costs.

In addition, across all three countries, healthcare insurance programmes do not, or do not fully, cover dental, hearing and vision examinations and care, or assistance with ADLs and IADLs. These omissions can be critical for older people, who are likely to lose health or abilities, and who often cannot pay for such care out of pocket. As we will show in the coming chapters, the precarity that older people can face under these three countries' policies is shaped not only by state reforms in the retirement and public health systems, but also by broader social transformations affecting the labour market (for example, an increase in unstable jobs) and families (for example, divorce rates, blended families and fewer children) (Lain et al, 2021).

Older people deploy several strategies to deal with economic insecurity. Continued labour market engagement is one. This is especially the case in the US, where the labour force participation rates for both men and women over 65 are projected to reach 21.8 per cent (25.9 per cent for men and 18.3 per cent for women) in 2026, up from 12.1 per cent in 1996 (16.9 and 8.6 per cent for men and women, respectively) (Bureau of Labor Statistics, 2017). Others relocate to new countries where the costs of living are lower. Some host countries, such as those that we discuss in this book, allow retirees to partake in their public healthcare schemes; and international agreements between home and host countries can enable retirees to receive their pensions at no or low cost. Still, moving abroad in retirement can be driven by factors other than economic security, though in such contexts, accessing retirement and healthcare protection abroad remains critical. Some retirees will relocate to maintain or improve a good lifestyle, while spending less to do so. However, escaping from social precarity based on older age is another factor, even for those who do not need to counter economic precarity. The prospect of a place where ageing has no effect on social status and where one can receive care as a valued person can also inspire retirement migration, as we will show in the following chapters.

4

Escaping economic precarity

Introduction

Helen was a 76-year-old divorcee who had resided in Mexico for several months at the time of her interview. As a retired professional, she had continued to work part-time until quite recently. Yet, her present income was low, being in the range of USD 2,200 a month.

Helen had lived in the Midwest of the US for most of her life. She was divorced when her sons were teenagers; her daughter was already in college. Her ex-husband had his own business, "stocks and money in the bank, I'm sure", and they owned two homes. However, she said that she "never pay[s] attention to things" and, as a result of that and some bad advice, received very little in her divorce settlement. She had a profession, so she did not push for alimony. She received one of their homes but no other money; the settlement stipulated that her ex-husband would pay for their sons' medical and educational expenses. However, this last provision was not honoured due to a legal loophole. In addition, she had some major, costly medical issues to resolve. As a result, she had to sell the house quickly to pay "for them to go to school and for all their needs". Had she been able to wait two more years, she said, she would have gotten twice as much money for her home, but she could not. What money she had left from the sale of her house she used to buy a car and put the rest (about USD 100,000) into stocks.

Before she moved to Mexico, Helen looked at her options and discussed these with one of her sons. She had thought about getting a recreational vehicle (RV) and travelling, parking it for a while in Mexico and then travelling in the US at other times:

> 'I'd never seen [a part of the US], and I have good friends [there], so I would go and visit them and see the [area]. But the RV I would want to live in and the RV I could afford were two different RVs. And also, I was realistic that an older woman alone was, you know – that wasn't practical.'

Helen also considered living on a boat but found that just as impractical. In search of affordable and competent medical care, she had visited the general area in Mexico where she now resides. Impressed, and at the encouragement of one of her sons, she decided to migrate. She now lives in a *casita* (small house), which she rents at a rate that she can afford on her monthly income.

The house has no central heating, and she says that the roads can wash out in the rain, but she is otherwise happy with her move. She has made many friends, goes out at night to hear music and is content, despite the problems with heating and other small complaints about her rental. She manages on what she has and does not look far into the future. She said that she has about USD 10,000 in the bank; she had more, but:

> 'I helped out my son with something, and so until he pays me back, I just have USD 10,000 saved. And … I trust it. … I don't need to [plan] … there's no way I can plan for or control what's going to happen in two years. I could be dead.'

Helen had worked well past full retirement age and yet found herself in a precarious financial situation. She had a profession but worked as a contract worker, which does not generate the kind of retirement security, in terms of occupational or other pensions, that she would have otherwise garnered. She had been married and even owned a home, but the exigencies of her divorce and obligations towards her children influenced financial decisions that contributed to her precarity.

Contrast Helen's experience with that of another couple within her community in Mexico. Carl and Joan, aged 71 and 72, respectively, moved to Mexico about 12 years prior to the interview. Both had been married previously, but they had been together more than 20 years, married for 14. Neither had children, nor were they particularly close to siblings; Joan had a niece with whom they visited once or twice a year.

Despite their different occupations and circumstances, both Carl's and Joan's employment prospects were influenced by age, which limited their opportunities and led them both to leave the labour market before they qualified for SS. As Carl described it: "I got kicked out of the workplace. [Joan] got kicked out with a bit of a parachute. Not so much for [a worker like me]." His description of the career in his field reflects the fast pace of change in that occupation, as well as the difficulty that older workers have in being valued or being taught new skills (Lain et al, 2019, 2021). Although he was aware that he had not kept up in the field, he ultimately attributed his job loss to ageism. He noted that being in his profession was great for a long time, as there was a shortage of workers with his expertise; however, the educational systems in other countries then began to generate skilled workers, which hurt his employment:

> 'So, the curves finally intersected, if you will, and suddenly it became the case that there were a lot more [trained workers] than there were jobs, and those people were half my age, much more up-to-date than I was and willing to work for half what I was getting. So, it was like,

"I'm seeing writing on the wall." I beat my head against it for a year or so. I had been in my previous position for approximately ten years and the one before that for approximately ten years. What I was able to find at that point was like two-week positions, and it was the most amazing thing. They had gotten to the point where they could roll you in for a two-week job, give you a 401K, give you healthcare, give you everything as if you were going to be there for a while, and then roll you off in all of two weeks. I just found that really amazing.'

After a series of temporary positions, he was laid off: "I knew exactly what was going on." His work life also made clear the ways in which job instability is a part of employment structures that occurs at the behest of employers.

Joan's earlier-than-planned retirement emerged from a different circumstance. She had backgrounds in two professional realms and wound up moving into what she described as marketing work in various capacities. She noted that she "did not get fired but saw the writing on the wall. ... You know, at 60 you don't go [laughing] [looking] for a new job." Her boss had been let go, and she could see what was happening. The company for which she worked was "merging and selling off bits ... and buying up bits, and um, it wasn't the same, they weren't hiring [highly educated workers], let's just say, anymore. They were getting cheaper labour", so she realised that "those of us who were the ones who had been around, we had more, we were expensive to keep around". Once her boss left, then, she felt that it was just a matter of time. Therefore, rather than wait, she decided to ask for a severance package. She had just landed a contract with an enormous international corporation:

> 'I have all the right people set up, I've got the Internet set up, I've got everything set up for this account, and I'd like to go out on that note. So, I'd like the package my boss got! [Laughs.] That's what I said! ... And I got the package ... you know, they wished me well and, um, I went out feeling good.'

Both Carl's and Joan's stories made clear that their advancing ages played a role in their ability to gain or keep employment, even for those who occupy more highly paid, professional positions. They differed in that Joan's job was higher status and she was doing well and opted to quit before being pushed out. However, she could see it coming, not just at her corporation, but among peers at other companies: "people who are working for corporations at that time were all kind of feeling that squeeze".

Joan's and Carl's stories differed tremendously not only from Helen's but also from those of many of the other migrants. They had money and a cushion, whereas most of the others did not. Although they felt pushed out of their jobs, they had options. In addition to Joan's severance package and whatever pensions they would eventually receive, Carl had just inherited some money, and they thought: " 'You know, we might be able to, kind of, just retire now, and we won't have to fight our way back into the workplace', which had changed a lot at that point."

Unlike others who had left the labour force before they could receive a national pension, Joan and Carl were not facing economic precarity. They appreciated that they could move to Mexico and have a very nice house and a comfortable life. Others, such as Stephanie, whom we discussed in Chapter 1, were no longer in the labour force and struggled to survive financially. So too were many of our respondents who retired early or, like Helen, well after full retirement age. We examine these experiences in greater depth in the following.

Retirement migration and economic precarity

Economic precarity in later life results from disadvantages accumulated over the life course that emerge from intersecting systems of inequalities (Dannefer, 2020; Grenier et al, 2021; Simmonds, 2021). Lain and colleagues (2019, 2021) argue that to analyse precarity as a 'lived experience', we need to consider at least three components of people's lives: the welfare state policies that shape their lives and the provisions on which they rely; their present and past positions in the labour market; and their household composition. The authors point to specific situations that can produce precarity in later life in these three spheres. First, precarious work conditions at older ages can result in unstable incomes, a greater risk of unemployment (and inability to find comparable re-employment) or being stuck in a position because of limited alternative employment options or insufficient welfare protection. These risks are rooted in the neoliberal labour market, and ageism in workplaces exacerbates these risks. Such precarity has tremendous impacts not only on income but also on well-being and identities (Lassus et al, 2015; Kalleberg, 2018; Lain et al, 2019).

Alongside this job insecurity is the increasingly precarious welfare state. In his examination of precarity in six rich democracies, Kalleberg (2018) makes clear that labour market insecurity can be heightened or ameliorated to a great extent by welfare state policies, not only in relation to employment but also, for example, in terms of such social protections as healthcare access, leaving workers in the UK in a better position than those in the US. In terms of older workers specifically, as we have noted, welfare states in the Global North have undergone major changes since the 1980s, shaped by policy makers' desire to reduce public expenses and leading to the withdrawal of the state from policies securing old age, among other things (see also Phillipson, 2021). According to Lain et al (2019), these transformations have forced a growing proportion of the population to work longer, which particularly disadvantages those groups – such as women – faced with higher risks of insecure working conditions in later life.

Finally, Lain and colleagues (2019, 2021) see the household playing a significant role in reducing or increasing precarity stemming from the interaction of the welfare state and the labour market. Major transformations in family life and household composition, typically due to divorce and remarriage, as well as such events as widowhood, and financial responsibility for other family members have an impact on families' economic stability and their abilities to deal with different risks occurring elsewhere. In this respect, divorced women and widows can be particularly at risk because, depending on how old age policies deal with women who may have relied on husbands for pensions, their marital trajectories can have strong, negative impacts on their financial resources. The authors also point to the major role that home ownership can play in providing security in later life. Those able to pay off mortgages can use their housing as an asset to reduce other economic risks around retirement age. Yet, this is not the case for those who still need to pay a mortgage, or are not owners at all, a situation made all the more dire in those regions where housing is quite expensive.

The three overlapping dimensions discussed by Lain et al (2019, 2021) – a precarious labour market, precarious welfare state and precarious household – played significant roles in our interviewees' experiences of migration. This was particularly the case for those whose decision to relocate was linked intricately to the search for more economic security. Most of these retirees left – or were forced out of – the labour market prior to reaching full retirement age. That is to say, a substantial number of our respondents either began collecting their pensions early or – and this was unexpected – were essentially 'not in the labour force'. This latter group was comprised of older, displaced workers unable to find comparable employment (often because of ageism) and who were no longer considered to be in the labour market, workers with disabilities, and, in general, people who had been employed in precarious jobs before leaving the labour market definitively. The prevalence of this precarious group likely reflected our interest in interviewing only those whose relocations to new countries was permanent; they did not spend part of their year in their home countries and a portion elsewhere. While some of them were able to collect benefits from their home country, most relied upon their private savings. In addition, some of those who reached full retirement age, such as Helen, had low pensions, such that they were still economically insecure. The expenses that our interviewees sought to reduce by relocating abroad varied, depending on their home country, but were generally linked to health, food, housing and energy costs. As we discuss more fully in Chapter 7, issues related to providing and receiving assistance in later life were also important for many. Finally, even though it could be lessened, for some of our respondents, economic precarity remained despite their migration. Single women were particularly subject to this and worried about their future needs for support.

Migration before full retirement age

The notion of international retirement migration assumes that people relocate to another country to live, bringing with them their state and other pension benefits. This differentiates them from other North – South migrants who have not reached retirement age and presumably relocate for paid work. Yet, we find that retirement migration also describes early retirees, in that it can also serve as a way for individuals to negotiate their transition to retirement before reaching full retirement age. In such a context, seeking economic security can play a significant role. This was the case among the retirement migrants who participated in our study. Among those of our interviewees who had left their home countries before reaching full retirement age, some went ahead and collected their pension benefits one to three years before full eligibility. As a result, their benefits were permanently reduced, and their ability to afford living costs in their home country was diminished. This was one reason why they sought to move to a place with a lower cost of living. Others had left the labour market before they could even collect early pensions. As a result, some had no income and lived on their savings, while others received occupational benefits, and one man used severance pay he had received when he lost his job. The reasons for early retirement varied but reflected situations often encountered by older workers: long-term unemployment; unsafe or unstable jobs; no options for better-paid work opportunities; and ageism by employers (Lassus et al, 2015; Lain et al, 2019). Health issues could add to these motivations.

Older people no longer in the workforce

Our study revealed a group about whom little has been written but who might be growing as labour market precarity increases. As noted earlier, job displacement or health can push some older works out of the labour market entirely, well before retirement age, placing them in a situation where they need to create a way to survive outside of paid work or a pension. In Spain, Stephanie had worked in low-paid jobs for several years before her health forced her to leave the labour market permanently, well before reaching retirement age. Likewise, Lorraine had divorced early and had a son to raise with only minimal financial help from her ex-husband. She worked a series of different low-paid jobs in different real estate companies while she lived in the US. In her 50s, she lost her job and was only able to cobble together short-term jobs; she tried self-employment as well, but was not able to do so successfully. She found herself unable to find any more paid work and decided to move to Costa Rica, even though she had not reached retirement age.

Both insecure employment and poor health played a role in the relocation of Joseph and his wife Sophie, aged 57 and 54, respectively, who had moved to Costa Rica one year before the interview. After losing his job in the service sector, Joseph had accumulated periods of unemployment and low-paying, unstable jobs, which ultimately prompted him to move out of the US. When we asked him how he had made the decision to relocate, Joseph answered:

> 'My previous job, I was very happy with, and I made pretty good money, and there was no reason for me to go anywhere. It was a comfortable living. It was when I lost that good job, and that I couldn't get a good job and I had to take half the amount of money, and I wasn't very happy, and I couldn't find anything really better. That's the reason.'

Joseph's experiences illustrate the difficulties that older workers face in trying to find employment: they not only take longer than younger workers to find new jobs, but those that they acquire also have lower pay and worse benefits (Lassus et al, 2015). In addition to Joseph's difficulty finding a job with decent wages, Sophie had also lost her job in a physically demanding profession due to poor health: "I stopped [working] because I threw my back out", she explained, "and it was severe enough that the doctor said that I could never go back to doing that [job]". She said that she would have been forced out of her job eventually, as her health constituted a liability for her employer: "I was ... seeing kind of the writing on the wall: that my career was probably over." Since she was not eligible for any state-sponsored benefits, she was left without an income. Both she and Joseph were unable to work: Sophie because of her health and Joseph due to suffering the fate of an older, unemployed worker. Yet, both were too young to collect pensions. Migrating presented them with a chance to deal with their economic precarity.

Migrants with an early-retirement pension

Economic precarity could affect retirement migrants who started to collect pensions before reaching full retirement age. Charlotte, a 63-year-old woman whom we met in Spain, exemplifies one outcome of such precarious employment well. She had retired before being eligible for a full public pension. She was divorced and had worked several years in low-paid and insecure employment in the UK. She had lost several jobs, due to what she and other interviewees called 'redundancy', a process whereby employers dismiss workers to reduce labour costs, often by substituting technology or by restructuring jobs to have other workers perform additional tasks.

Seeing no way to secure her income through stable, well-paid employment, Charlotte retired early and relocated to Spain less than a year before the interview took place. She spoke of the different jobs that she had held, as well as the instability and the ageism she had faced on the labour market as an older employee:

> 'I worked [as an] office manager. And then the company made everybody redundant, so I had to go away and find something, and I got a job as a secretary in an agency. But that was my last job. ... I was there for about six months, but then the [company] got rid of all the secretaries 'cause the computers were recording everything, it was all digital, so the secretaries all went. And then I [joined a temp agency] again, and I got another job. ... Then, that office closed, everybody was made redundant. ... Then, I got [another] job until January last year. ... I left because my boss was a bully. ... He was picking on my work, finding fault with my work while there was nothing wrong with my work, but he just had to. He was very disrespectful of me as well. ... Young enough to be my son, and I felt it so difficult. In the end, it was making me ill. So, this is when I made [the decision to move to Spain].'

In Costa Rica, Jenny, a 63-year-old woman from the US, had left her job earlier due to work-related health issues, a context that Lain et al (2021) also discuss. She had worked in education, and although she had enjoyed her work for most of her career, the last decade prior to retirement had become increasingly stressful. She developed anxiety, backaches and insomnia, and resorted to daily medications. This made her want to retire as soon as possible, but she had few savings and could not afford to retire until she was eligible to collect benefits. She retired early, when she was 62, but her subsequently reduced benefit was not enough to live on in the US. Jenny was divorced and had no children. Her ex-husband owned a house in a village in Costa Rica, where many other US migrants lived. Facing the economic consequences of her early retirement, a couple of months before the interview took place, she relocated to Costa Rica to live in one of two apartments in her ex-husband's house. She hoped to teach English and Spanish to augment her income and, like Helen, felt she could manage if she were careful:

> 'Yes, right now, I'm comfortable because I'm living very modestly, very frugally. I don't have a car. ... The place I live is paid for, so I don't have rent. Yeah, I'm fine. Financially, I'm ok unless I have, you know, a disaster, like a medical disaster, but even then, I can go to the hospital here. I have insurance. ... I don't live extravagantly; I don't live

grandiose. I don't wear fancy clothes. I live economically within my money. ... I try to live on USD 1,000 a month, and it's very doable.'

However, she felt anxious about how she would manage her future.

In Mexico, Maria had migrated with her spouse Jessie before she was eligible for a pension (Maria was only 59 at the time of the interview) and when Jessie was able to collect an early benefit (at age 63). Maria did not have a steady job but worked in a variety of capacities, all related to design or art, as opportunities came along. Jessie's job had involved outdoor work, and his health had begun to suffer as a result. After some scares, they decided that his income from work was not worth the cost of his health. He needed to stop. They had listened to an audiotape years prior on how to live cheaply and calculated that they could use the equity in their US home to buy a house in Mexico and pay off their debts. Therefore, when they decided that he would work no more – as Maria put it, "regardless, he was going to stop working" – they moved. As Maria could not collect benefits yet, they lived on Jessie's reduced benefit and supplemented that by renting out a room of their house to tourists. All told, their income was less than USD 2,000 a month.

Like the examples of Jenny, along with Jose and Maria, many of the early retirees whom we interviewed lived on little or no income outside of savings or a reduced pension; any supplementary income was small and not guaranteed. This was in contrast to respondents who had migrated after their full retirement income began. Still, some of the latter respondents also mentioned the issue of economic precarity as an important motivation for relocating abroad. In the next section, we turn our attention to those who moved after reaching full retirement age.

Migration after reaching full retirement age

In contrast to the situations presented earlier, some interviewees had remained active in the labour market until they received full retirement benefits. Leaving the labour market at retirement age was either legally mandated, as in Switzerland, or voluntary. However, even among those who worked until retirement age, benefits could be low. Faced with bad jobs, on the one hand, and with poor re-employment prospects and welfare safety net, on the other (Lain et al, 2019), these older workers had entered retirement financially insecure. Like the early retirees, a significant portion of them had been concerned about their ability to afford living in their home country due to a 'precarious welfare state', in which 'individuals [are] not provided with adequate financial security in the absence of employment' (Lain et al, 2019: 2225). These interviewees had not faced precarious ends to their careers, but their work histories and earnings had resulted in a retirement pension that did not provide them with enough economic security to stay in their home country. In contrast to those retirees who were happy to be in a new country because they would not need to spend down their wealth as quickly, these migrants were at risk of having too few economic resources to survive.

In Spain, the couple of Dan (age 66) and Irène (age 58) had left Switzerland just after Dan reached retirement age, less than a year before the interview took place. Both had been employed in the service sector. When her husband retired, Irène had also stopped working. Although they had been able to work until Dan was entitled to a full pension, retirement had significantly reduced their income. In contrast to interviewees who owned a house in the UK or the US, they had not paid for their house in full when they reached retirement, a common situation in Switzerland – the country with the lowest rate of home ownership in Europe (Balmer and Gerber, 2018). Therefore, they still had a monthly mortgage, a situation likely to reinforce precarity in later life (Lain et al, 2019; Ong et al, 2019). Faced with their inability to bear this financial burden for the long run, they sold their house and looked to relocate to a place with a lower cost of living. Spain fit the bill: it was both cheaper than Switzerland and not far geographically, which was important, they said, as their children needed frequent material and emotional support.

Like Dan, Georgette, a 65-year-old Swiss woman, had left the labour market at full retirement age, but her benefits were insufficient to ensure economic security. She was divorced and, like most women in Switzerland, had always worked part-time in low-paying jobs while caring for her children (Madero-Cabib, 2016). The need to reduce her living expenses motivated her to migrate to Spain. For her, living in Switzerland as a retiree meant economic insecurity: "How can I put this? Staying in Switzerland [with] 2,800 Swiss francs [per month], you don't do a lot. … Living here is cheap. But it is tight."

We found similar situations among the US interviewees who had retired when eligible for a full pension. For instance, Luke and Beatrice, aged 66 and 68, respectively, had worked most of their lives running a small business, from which they garnered an income but no wealth. In planning for their retirement, they realised that they would not be able to afford to live in the US in the long term. They made clear that seeking economic security for their later years was the main reason for their migration to Costa Rica. Moving had been hard for Beatrice, who missed her friends and her previous community. However, she felt that it was necessary, as she explained:

> 'Everything is getting more expensive [in the US]. Power, water … everything. So, we looked at the future and saw it's only going to get more expensive. … It's cheaper to live here than in the US, and it's a

nicer area. ... So, the bottom line is that, financially, it's cheaper here and less expensive. And the quality of life is also very good. ... We have ... Social Security, and we have investments which support us here. It's enough to support us.'

The situation of Laura (age 74) combines many of the themes described earlier. She and her husband had lived in Mexico for six years at the time of the interview. Both had been married previously and had lost some financial security through their divorces. However, in addition, her husband, who was 69, had become disabled and had to stop working prior to full retirement age. They had also spent much of their savings on rehabilitating his son, who had come close to dying due to alcoholism. At the behest of a family member who lived there, they had purchased the house in Mexico years before they moved there, when it was quite inexpensive. In the meantime, they did not own a home in the US but were paying rent, which they found increasingly expensive, especially after his disability. They moved to Mexico to save money, and Laura spent two more years working in the US (and living with a friend) until she reached full retirement age. They had no savings and only SS benefits, which were not sufficient for the costs of living in the US. Divorce and financial responsibilities for an adult child drained their retirement savings; even though she worked until full retirement age, her relatively low earnings translated into a relatively low pension. Their combined benefits left them financially insecure.

Economic precarity was a major motivation for most of our respondents to migrate. The insecurities that they faced in their home countries were often the result of working lives that were shaped by long-term unstable and low-paid jobs coming to an end. In some cases, this was compounded by health issues or, in the case of women, major care duties, which had challenged the respondents' abilities to do paid work and maintain economic security. Even those women whose work histories are not intermittent are typically paid less than men (Gottfried, 2013), and this influenced their incomes. Finally, some interviewees – including those who had worked until they reached full retirement eligibility – faced economic precarity because their income had been low throughout their work histories, and all the welfare states in question calculate retirement benefits based on earnings, thereby reproducing labour market inequalities.

Migrants who lost money in the 2007–08 recession

As several scholars have noted (for example, Lain et al, 2019; Grenier et al, 2021; Phillipson, 2021), major financial crises can dramatically increase precarity in later life. At the same time, such websites as International Living acknowledge this and promote migration as a strategy to deal with it. For instance, Croucher (2022: 175) reports the experience of one American that was documented on that site:

> 'Like millions of others during the 2008 recession, Diane and I found ourselves struggling to survive when my executive-level job disappeared and the equity in our home quickly vanished. ... The global economic meltdown had forced its way into our family and the consequences were painful and very personal.' (Murray, 2016)

Reflecting this situation, the insecure positions of several interviewees resulted, at least in part, from the 2007–08 financial crisis. In Spain, Alma and Ivan, a formerly well-off couple aged 69 and 63, respectively, when we first interviewed them, had lost a lot of money consequent to the crash when they were in their 50s. Fortunately, they had been able to sell a house that they owned in the UK and moved to Spain to buy a cheaper house and live with the money they had made from this transaction. As Ivan explained:

> 'With the [2007–08] crisis, I lost a lot of money. I lost about half a million [pounds sterling], probably, in the crisis. So, we were left just with our house and the one flat from before we had our house. So, from a house ... and five flats, we went to one house and one flat. So, we sold that. ... With that money that we got there, we started again here.'

At the time of the interview, they were living on Alma's pension benefits, which they hoped would allow them to wait until Ivan reached full retirement age to collect his own pension. They maintained that their financial situation would have been quite difficult had they stayed in England.

Other interviewees who were not yet eligible to collect pension benefits had lost their job, house or savings in the 2007–08 recession. In some cases, this added to their economic disadvantages or health issues. Diana, a 60-year-old woman from the US whom we interviewed in Costa Rica, provides one example. Diana and her husband had lost their entire retirement savings (USD 500,000) in the recession. Further, Diana, who worked in the health sector for 15 years, had had to quit for health reasons and before she had worked long enough to be eligible for her employers' pension plan. As her husband did not have high earnings, they needed to find a way to spend less. After weighing their options, they decided to sell their house in the US and buy a cheaper one in Costa Rica. Their house needed repairs, and Diana left the US to work on this while her husband kept running his business in the US. They planned that her husband would eventually either improve his business and stabilise their income or join her in Costa Rica. Thus, Diana's migration decision was a strategy to address the economic precarity they were facing in their retirement years by reducing their spending as much as possible:

'The reason [I came to Costa Rica] was [that my husband and I] can't afford to stay in the United States. Having our own business, we were not able ... when we were younger, to put money away. So, we just started, really, in 2003 to 2008–2009. ... Then we lost it. So, all we have is our Social Security, which between the two of us, should be, at full [retirement age], about USD 2,800 a month. But then they take out Medicare, they take out taxes, so you're talking about ... USD 2,000 to USD 2,100 a month for two people to live on.'

Diana linked her and her husband's financial precarity to the broader neoliberal welfare policies in the US, stressing that "everybody says, 'Save for retirement, save for retirement.' Well, that's all well and good", she commented, "but if you have children you have to feed ... sometimes you just don't have it".

Retirement migrants with precarious households

Reflecting observations made by Lain and colleagues (2019), the consequences of precarious jobs and insufficient welfare state provision can be made worse by household situation, typically by marital changes (for example, divorce, widowhood and remarriage), or financial responsibilities for other family members. Providing and receiving care to or from family members earlier or later in life was another issue that we found to shape retirement migration and precarity experiences, one that is significantly driven by gender.

Some women in our sample were either divorced or widowed, and some carried out significant care work in their families, both before and after migration. Due to their caring role, labour market discrimination and, in some countries, poor or no (such as in the US) public childcare provisions, they had low incomes and thus few resources in retirement. Stephanie, whose situation we described earlier, had begun her work life as a secretary but lost her job several years ago. She then occupied a low-paid and insecure job in the public sector in England before becoming disabled. Her situation was made even more difficult because she had children and her mother to care for. Others, such as Helen, with whom we opened this chapter, had worked in professional occupations and well past retirement age. However, her divorce impacted her economic status negatively, such that her family financial responsibilities left her with little in savings to go along with her small benefit. Helen's situation was compounded by the fact that she worked as a self-employed contract worker, as did another US divorcee, Maggie, which impacted their national pensions. Neither Helen and Maggie nor Stephanie had enough income to have financial security in later life.

The living costs that matter: variations by welfare state

Like other scholars of retirement migration (for example, Hayes, 2018a), we found that participants had prepared for their relocation over months or years by assessing the economic advantages and risks of moving abroad, and by comparing these across different possible host countries. Most of them had looked for information using websites targeting North – South migrants, like International Living or A Place in the Sun. They had also visited websites that especially targeted retirement migrants and online networks (usually Facebook groups) of retirement migrants or other expatriates living in their future host country to gather more information and make initial contacts.

For instance, before moving to Costa Rica, Damian and his wife had used the Internet to study the advantages of relocating to another country. They had compared several in Central America and had found that Costa Rica was inexpensive, especially in relation to food, healthcare and housing. They had contacted state organisations in their home and host countries to learn how to receive their pension abroad and how to access public health insurance in their host country.

Most of our interviewees had considered the costs of travelling back and forth between their present and future countries. Many had family in the former, and some relied on healthcare in their home countries due either to personal preference or a lack of services in their host country (see also Chapter 7). Our respondents in Mexico and Spain could travel cheaply; they mentioned the availability of low-cost airlines as a major advantage of their new home. Things were a bit different for those in Costa Rica, where flights to the US were more expensive.

Although our respondents shared similar concerns regarding travel costs and accessibility, they also focused on some different expenditures. These variations related to their home countries and the different welfare state benefits that they did or did not receive.

British migrants

Recalling British welfare state policies for later life, the main areas of concern for retirees were pension benefit levels and the ability to access the UK's universal free healthcare in Spain. In terms of the former, and thinking about surviving on meagre pensions, British interviewees generally talked about problems related to the costs of food and travel in the UK, as well as heating. In Spain, they did not have to pay as much for heating, both because the cost was relatively cheap and because the weather was warm. However, winter was particularly cold during the time of our fieldwork in 2017, and this had created stress among some of our respondents, who were preoccupied by the effects of this unusual weather on their finances.

For British participants, healthcare costs had not previously been a concern because their citizenship had granted them access to free healthcare in Spain, an advantage based upon agreements between countries of the EU. This had changed, however, with the vote for the UK to leave the EU ('Brexit'), which had taken place a couple of months before our field study in Spain. As a result, they were more worried about their future healthcare needs. For instance, Sylvie considered free healthcare to be a condition for her and her husband's ability to live in Spain:

> 'The only reason I can think where we would go back [to the UK] would be if Brexit causes us such problems that the UK government would not pay for [our healthcare] here. Then we would have to go back because we have private health insurance [in Spain], but it doesn't cover for pre-existing conditions, and … my husband has a few pre-existing conditions [which are not covered by the private insurance].'

Like Sylvie, British respondents worried about the consequences of Brexit, as they could not always afford to pay for healthcare out of pocket or to obtain private insurance.

In addition to future access to healthcare, British retirees were concerned about the negative impact of the Brexit vote on the value of the pound, in particular, whether it might decrease their pension benefits. As Alma put it:

> 'It's cheaper to live here. Because the … tax that we pay in England, we would pay nearly £2,000 a year, and here we pay £300–400. So, lots of difference there. A lot of things like that, it's much too dire to live in England. But now that our pensions are getting less, it's not so good as it was because food is getting dire for us, the electricity is expensive here, gas is.'

Later in the interview, Alma and her husband Ivan spoke again about their post-Brexit financial concerns. Ivan noted that pre-Brexit, their life in Spain had been very comfortable, but now, the value of the pound was worrisome. As a result, as Alma noted: "Our pension is getting to be less every month. And also, we don't know if we're gonna have enough [income]. I think we'll be allowed to stay, but will we still have … free healthcare?"

Affording housing, food and heating was a concern for the British interviewees due to their sometimes very low incomes. For them, healthcare was not an issue so far, thanks to their health insurance coverage in the UK and in the EU. However, the Brexit vote had brought new forms of uncertainties regarding their ability to live at lower costs in Spain in the future, as their healthcare coverage was put into question and their pensions were losing value.

Swiss migrants

Unlike the British retirees, Swiss people do not benefit from free healthcare, but as with the UK and the US, pensions are related to earnings over the work life. Thus, Swiss interviewees mostly mentioned healthcare and housing – given its high cost – as the financial challenges they faced in their home country. Many struggled to afford the mandatory Swiss health insurance premiums necessary for accessing healthcare, as well as the expenses not covered by insurance, such as dental or eye care. Housing costs were mentioned as a problem by both those who rented and those who owned property, all of whom were still paying a mortgage. In this regard, Swiss retirees differed from their UK or US counterparts, as most of the latter interviewees had managed to have built up a fair amount of equity in their homes. According to Jean-Charles and Marlyse, aged 70 and 63, respectively, it would have been difficult to live in Switzerland in retirement, mostly because of the combined health and housing costs:

Marlyse:	You must calculate that if you live in Switzerland … the insurance for both of us is already 1,000 francs.
Jean-Charles:	It would have been more difficult. … You would have had to calculate more carefully. … Keep a budget.
Marlyse:	Paying rent for the apartment.
Jean-Charles:	It would have been difficult.

Georgette also spoke of her difficulty in affording housing on her retirement income in Switzerland. She had not made enough money to buy an apartment or a house when she was working, and the apartment she rented while she was employed had become too expensive in retirement. The only option was to live with her mother in an apartment her mother owned, something that she found difficult to do. She lived in Spain with a Swiss partner she had met some years ago, who owned an apartment there. However, she had kept an address in Switzerland and still paid her healthcare premiums and co-payments. Those already took away about 20 per cent of her income.

For the Swiss migrants, affording housing and health insurance was a major issue due to their insufficient retirement pensions, as well as the high prices of housing and of the mandatory health insurance. The important expenditures resulting from these costs made all other needs (such as food, heating and so on) difficult to afford.

US migrants

Based on pension benefits that reflect earnings, the US participants found that costs of living were high for retirees in the US. The few respondents who did not own houses were concerned about those costs; however, the majority spoke of healthcare as the major financial challenge they faced in their home country. Those who were over 65 years old had Medicare, but this only covered a portion of their expenses. As a programme, Medicare covers 65 per cent of healthcare costs for beneficiaries. Co-payments can be quite costly and represent a large portion of discretionary income for those who are most financially insecure (Federal Interagency Forum on Aging-Related Statistics, 2020). Further, early retirees had either never had health insurance, lost it when they lost their job or paid for very expensive private plans. All struggled with the costs of paying insurance premiums, as well as deductibles and co-insurance. For Beatrice, this had been a major reason why their economic situation was insecure in the US:

> 'The problem in the States, because there's no healthcare for everybody and it's expensive, if you're a young family and you don't have medical insurance, if you get sick, you can lose everything. And for all the older families, you've worked all your life and you have a big medical problem, you can lose everything you've worked all your life [for] just to pay for your medical bills.'

Damian and his wife had a similar view. They had retired early after realising that her professional situation had deteriorated over the previous few years. She owned a business but did not have sufficient clients to make it viable anymore, which spelled a consequent reduction in the couple's financial stability. Yet, they were too young to be eligible for a retirement pension or Medicare. Damian found healthcare costs for him and his wife to be so high that little money was left for other basic needs:

> 'If I stayed in the United States, I couldn't afford [healthcare]. ... We can live down here for less than USD 2,000 a month. For both of us. That includes health insurance, food, everything. Where if I retired in the United States, if I had to get my own insurance, it would cost me USD 1,000 per month, just for that. ... And then I'd have to come up with money for a house, food, entertainment and everything else. It's very expensive to live in the United States, especially on a fixed income. I have no income anymore. What I have saved in the bank is all I have.'

As these quotes suggest, the expensive healthcare system in the US has significant impacts in later life. The fact that there is no universal healthcare insurance before 65 years old presents a risk of not having access to healthcare or contracting major debts for healthcare reasons, especially for workers faced with insecure ends of careers and forced to retire sooner. Medicare can only be accessed after age 65 and offers limited coverage, and affording more healthcare security can be a problem. In such contexts, retiring abroad can improve healthcare affordability, even though in some retirement migrants' locations, the healthcare systems can be limited (see Chapter 7).

In sum, a major concern for our retirement migrants was healthcare coverage, and this varied in relation to the welfare states in both home and host countries. Due to the way that their healthcare policies work, US and Swiss interviewees were the most concerned with these expenses. The Swiss struggled to pay for their mandatory health insurance premiums and the costs of care not covered by the insurance. Depending on their age, the US interviewees had either no public insurance or limited coverage in their home country, while the medical costs and co-payments were sometimes very expensive. The situation of British retired migrants differed. At the time of our interviews in 2016–17, they had free access to healthcare in Spain, regardless of age, as they did in the UK. For them, affording healthcare was not a problem in either their home or host countries.

In addition, as a result of their labour market histories, as well as family, healthcare and retirement policies, the single retired women in our studies were often more economically disadvantaged than the other retirement migrants were. Several of them relied on their ability to make some extra money, sometimes through the help of a man (such as an ex-partner or a friend), as well as by renting out a room, delivering goods or services, or teaching private language lessons. Jenny – a US woman in Costa Rica, whom we mentioned earlier – gave English lessons to augment her income. Lorraine, another US respondent in Costa Rica, had developed a small real estate company in Costa Rica in an attempt to complement her very low SS. However, she was not very successful in this effort, and she feared going bankrupt when we interviewed her. In Spain, Jane worked some as an interpreter for the town government.

When economic precarity remains

Living abroad helped many of our interviewees reduce their expenses and live decent qualities of life; however, as the previous discussion about Brexit suggests, their situation often remained precarious. A slight change in their circumstances could diminish their financial security. In this sense, precarity is dynamic, and our respondents expressed both relief at being able to live with less money and anxiety about an uncertain future. For instance, Joseph and Sophie, a US couple, were among those out of the labour force but too young for retirement benefits. They moved to Costa Rica in search of economic security but had not been able to stabilise finances in their new country. They had lived there for a year at the time of the interview and had lost money due to several unexpected events. They had bought a relatively large house with three extra bungalows that they hoped to rent to tourists, but they found that renting the bungalows did not garner them enough money. Joseph, who had been the leader in the couple's decision to move abroad, felt bad about the situation, as his wife had first been reluctant about the idea to live far away from her children:

> 'Right now, we don't have a lot of extra money so … the anxiety is really … maybe I feel guilty, or I feel so more so because of my wife. You know, she has a new grandbaby. … I mean, we [came here] for the right reasons, but now that things have changed … it had to be somebody's idea to come here, right? … It was my idea, so it's kind of … I feel guilty about that maybe a little bit. … For healthcare, we applied for residency. … So, when you get residency here, you can apply for the national health. So, right now, we're just hoping that nothing happens between now and then because we have nothing right now.'

Going back to the US was financially unthinkable. They lacked the economic resources to live there, as they had invested all their money in the migration. Yet, to stay in Costa Rica, they needed a form of economic stability that they had not yet found.

For the British respondents in Spain, the Brexit vote was also a game changer, as it produced new forms of precarity or reinforced their insecurities – something that has been the subject of recent investigations (Benson et al, 2022). Such respondents were unsure whether they would continue to enjoy free healthcare; this uncertainty created new anxieties for them, as many could not afford to migrate back to their home country. As Nina, for instance, explained: "To go back to the UK to buy a property now would be – it's very expensive and very difficult. … After the Brexit vote, and we just don't know what's going to happen." Likewise, Jim found his situation much more insecure than before. He regretted having sold his house in the UK because he was worried about what he would do. In fact, several interviewees expressed similar worries. First, if Brexit caused them to lose their free healthcare, many felt that the Spanish public health plan might be difficult to access due to their age and health conditions, and would be more expensive as a result. Second, they were concerned that should they not be able to stay in Spain after Brexit, they might lose money in trying to sell their house in Spain, especially if other British migrants tried to do the same, thus depressing house prices. In addition, housing prices in the UK had grown significantly, so going through such a transaction would present a major economic loss for them.

Finally, single women were especially influenced by constant economic precarity, despite migration. The money they had to live on was especially low due to the low-paid, part-time or unstable jobs that had marked their working lives and that shaped their retirement finances. Whether they were never married, were divorced or were widowed, the gender division of labour and labour market discrimination had kept most of our single female respondents from accumulating sufficient retirement resources, and they were particularly reliant on inadequate welfare state provisions. Although migrating helped, it did not represent a permanent solution or offer them any strong sense of security.

Conclusion

Many of our interviewees had experienced labour market precarity: job instability leading to earlier than desired retirement; labour market displacement altogether; or low earnings. They lost their jobs as older workers and were unable to find comparable employment, or they had health issues that pushed them out of the labour market. Living in a welfare state where such insecurity is only partially addressed, at best, or where retirement benefit levels are based on earnings prompted their migration. Their movement to a new country addressed the economic risks they faced as older workers and retirees. Living in a cheaper country stretched their incomes further.

Those retirement migrants who had left or lost their jobs when fully eligible for benefits and had relocated abroad were in a different position, though many still faced economic precarity. They received full retirement pensions, but their lifetime earnings did not garner them large amounts, and few had occupational pensions or savings. Interviewees mentioned being unable to afford housing, heating and food in their home countries, and they made clear that these problems could be solved by moving abroad. As many scholars suggest (for example, Lain et al, 2019; Grenier et al, 2021; Phillipson, 2021), economic crises, such as the 2007–08 recession, can also significantly reduce economic security in later life, and this event also precipitated migration for several of our interviewees. Finally, owning a house or an apartment can constitute a significant asset for security in retirement; having done so improved the financial situation of some interviewees who had been able to use the sale of their property to improve their economic security abroad.

Differences among our interviewees' experiences related directly to the welfare state policies in their home and host countries. Respondents were especially concerned with being able to access healthcare, especially those from the US and Switzerland. In such contexts, the host country could offer a solution by providing people who officially reside in the country with low-cost public healthcare coverage or fairly inexpensive private insurance or medical care costs.

Finally, although migration enabled many of our respondents to better their economic position, their relocation was only a partial solution. Precarity is dynamic, and even small changes in such areas as politics or health could change their situations for the worse. This was especially true for the single female retirement migrants, who were especially likely to continue facing precarity in their host country. The accumulation of insecure or low-paid jobs and care duties over the life course tended to result in a retirement with little income.

While many interviewees had moved abroad as a way to address economic insecurity, 30 per cent of them were like Carl and Joan, who had more income and did not express concerns about their ability to afford living in their home country (though they might have noted concerns about their ability to do so cheaply). Still, they sought to reduce their costs of living, which relocating abroad allowed them to do, and they cited economics as a factor in their move as well. In addition, as we will show in Chapter 5, all our respondents, regardless of economic situation, felt more included abroad than in their home countries.

5

Escaping ageism

Introduction

Joseph and Margaret, both aged 63, are an American married couple of 34 years. They retired early and have lived in Mexico for the past four years. Margaret worked as a high-school teacher and principal; Joseph worked in a managerial capacity for a non-profit organisation. Both had grown up on the West Coast and by the ocean, and had hoped to stay there. However, despite their professional backgrounds and middle-class status, by their late 50s, they began to see that the cost of living in their city ruled out a decent life there. They still had a mortgage to pay on their house, and they described themselves as living paycheque to paycheque. Moving to Mexico allowed them to live debt-free and still be by the ocean, as well as close enough to family (their son, siblings and a mother) that they could visit.

Part of what they enjoyed about Mexico was the way that they were treated by the local populations. As Joseph said:

> 'I don't think they see us as retirees. … They just see people that live here. … I think that's the beauty of it. … I think that's a product of culture, as well, down here. … You know that … the older generation is thought of, and cared for, and included … as they would do any other member of their family.'

He contrasted what he perceived as respect for older people in Mexico with what he saw in the US. Reflecting an awareness of inequalities, Margaret expanded on this feeling of inclusion as 'just people', juxtaposing this to the feelings of invisibility that older women face in the US:

> 'I think that one of the things that I sometimes experience in the United States, as an older woman, is the feeling of being invisible. Like I can, even in stores … that happens, and it's like amazing to me that I'm, like, "Wow, I've just asked you a question and you're then helping somebody behind me" … you know, it's like we become invisible. I don't feel invisible at all here, at all. … That's a difference that I've experienced.'

Social precarity and ageism

Although retirement migration can help to overcome the financial insecurities that some older people face in countries of the Global North, we find that relocating abroad also allows retirees to cope with another dimension of precarity not generally discussed: the *social precarity* resulting from ageism. That is to say, retirement migrants face the prospect of exclusion due to their advancing age.

Chapter 4 made clear the wide age range of our retirement migrants; many were not yet of retirement age, and thus ageism might not seem to threaten them. In addition to the fact that Margaret, introduced earlier, is only 63 and speaks of ageism, we offer two observations to provide context and clarify our argument. First, privileges tend to be invisible to those who have them, often only recognised if they begin to disappear. For instance, research on men who transitioned to being women found that they became aware of their male privilege when they received different, more negative treatment in the workplace as women – even when they have not changed jobs during their transition (Schilt, 2006). Second, this example shows that privilege can be temporary, and such is the case with age relations. It is often only when they can no longer 'pass' for being younger that many older people realise that they had unearned advantages based on age. Age relations are unique, in that everyone starts from a position of privilege, that is, 'not old', and thus learns ageism at a young age. As a result, many people struggle to resist ageing – to avoid being seen as old – as they do not want to occupy that 'other' status. This widespread repulsion and fear of growing older that fuels the anti-ageing industry is not only internalised (Levy, 2003); it is also evident in social discourse that labels older people a 'problem' that needs to be solved – a 'silver tsunami' that represents a national disaster and will wreak havoc on society (Calasanti, 2020). Further, it is embedded in social practices that, for instance, relegate older bodies to institutional facilities.

This ageism underlies what we are calling 'social precarity': the risk of social exclusion beyond the economic exclusion that retirement can bring. As we discussed in Chapter 1, as people in the Global North age, they face the risk of losing not just social status but also personhood, full adulthood with rights and autonomy, social connection, and value. As Joseph notes in his praise of Mexicans, older people just want to be seen as people – not 'othered'. When and how such marginalisation occurs varies by context, and it often happens slowly. Generally, we do not become 'old' overnight. It is the increased risk of being excluded because of age that older people confront and that many of our interviewees experienced or anticipated.

As with other inequalities, such as those based on gender, race or ethnicity, the subordinate group is either invisible or too visible. The skills and experiences of older people can go overlooked, not only in the workplace but also in other realms. At the same time, they become too visible when they are cast as beneficiaries from, rather than contributors to, their economies; any dependence is framed as a detraction from the greater good (see Chapter 3). Other systems of inequality, such as that based on gender, intersect with age relations. For instance, since older women face both gender and age-based discrimination, labour market discrimination emerges for them sooner, as their skills are valued even less than men's and their appearance marks them as old and socially invisible sooner (Calasanti, 2005; McMullin and Berger, 2006). At 63, Margaret had already begun to feel her invisibility in some public spaces.

In this chapter, we show how the ageism in our interviewees' home countries led them to feel excluded or to anticipate this, and how they found that they were valued in their new countries, rather than burdens. Avoiding ageism and social exclusion was not their primary motivation for migrating; however, finding that they were not marginalised in their new countries based on their age emerged as an important aspect of their happiness. Furthermore, the apparent absence of ageism mattered regardless of our respondents' class. That is to say, although ageism can reinforce the social precarity that older people with lower incomes experience, it also affects those with greater economic resources, even though the latter may have the ability to forestall being seen as old.

We begin the chapter with our respondents' accounts of being considered burdens in their home countries, which they contrast to their perception of being valued as contributors in Spain, Costa Rica and Mexico. We highlight the experiences of older women, who felt more visible and safe than they had felt at home. Then, we discuss the advantages retirement migrants have found in residing among age peers. We discuss the internalised ageism that many respondents demonstrated, which we take to suggest that their avoidance of social precarity is, at best, incomplete. In the conclusion, we summarise our findings while also suggesting that the extent to which retirement migrants avoid social precarity based on ageism is unclear.

Visible and valuable

The ageist view of older people as burdens on the state appeared in the narratives of many interviewees, even if some felt that this depiction did not relate to themselves. As we discussed in Chapter 3, they had received such messages through mass media, in political discourses and interpersonally in their home countries. Although the content of these ageist messages varied, respondents spoke of depictions of older people as burdens in all their home welfare states. Most contrasted this dismissive and negative treatment of older people to the welcome and regard that they received in Spain, Costa Rica and Mexico. They pointed to the respectful way that younger people talked to them, the attention that they showed to their needs and the ways in which they tried to make them feel comfortable. They had observed this difference in public spaces (such as restaurants, shops and banks) and believed that it resulted from cultural differences between home and host countries: as Joseph stressed at the start of this chapter, older people were perceived as important members of society in the latter compared to their home states, where they were often ignored and invisible. Their visibility in their host country called forth special treatment; their older appearance did not make them feel stigmatised. For instance, in Costa Rica, several interviewees explained that younger people treated older people with deference, giving attention to their potential physical or other challenges, while this was not the case in their home country. Banks were a typical location where these US interviewees observed this, as Beatrice and Luke, a US couple, explained:

Luke: In Costa Rica, I think the retirees are treated [well]. When you go to the bank, if you're a pensioner, then you don't wait in line. … I went to pay my property taxes. … I stand in line, and I wait. And I had four people in front of me and I'm waiting there, and the woman in front of me said to me: 'Do you want to go first?' … because I guess I'm old and grey. … She figured I was an old pensioner. So, I think here, they treat pensioners and old people better [than in the US].

Beatrice: Yeah, they wouldn't do that in the States.

Luke: No … you don't get any benefits from being old [in the US]. You wait in the back of the line just like anyone else.

Julien, another US citizen, had a similar experience:

'If I go into the bank … I walk up to the front because I'm a senior. And there was one place I went into and I didn't see anything, but somebody walked up to me and said: "Here." And they handed me their number, which was soon coming up, and they took my number … so I wouldn't have to wait. … That's what they do here for the elderly people. They respect the elderly people. … [T]here's … nothing like that in the US in a bank. You wait your turn.'

The respect and deference shown to older people was a consistent theme in our interviews and was contrasted to the ageism in home countries. Alma and her husband Ivan had left the UK more than 15 years ago to live in Spain. Five years ago, Alma fell ill and needed a significant amount of care. She and her husband had decided to go back to the UK, where he had children, in order to ensure that he would not be alone should she not recover. Luckily, her physical conditions improved after some time, and the couple made the decision to return to Spain to live. During her interview, Alma asserted that families took care of their older members in Spain, in contrast to the UK, where older people were treated as burdens: "They love their old people here", she said; "Most old people here live with the family, they don't live in homes. The family looks after them." However, she also pointed to the broader treatment of older people in Spain, not just by family members: "People are just lovely; they are very respectful towards old people", whereas "They call you names in Britain. 'Oh, look at you, fat old cow.' It's horrible."

Younger retired migrants expressed similar thoughts. Claire and Jeremy, a US couple in Costa Rica, also found that younger people in their host country showed more respect to older people than at home. Claire said that, "What I see is old people treated with more respect and deference here. So, I would have to say … I have felt very welcomed here." Upon further questioning, she speculated that the welcome she experienced was influenced, in part, by the political rhetoric of welcoming US retirees. However, she felt it went further:

> 'I think it's also larger than that; I think it's their attitude towards older people actually. … You just see it. … You will see them with old people in front of the line. … You see it in people holding the elbows of old people as they're walking. … They're just much kinder to … the elderly here.'

Interviewees in Spain also felt that their age status was more valued and garnered more respect than in their home countries. As in Costa Rica, they felt more welcomed than at home, and they thought that younger people did not consider older people to be a burden. As Jane, a British woman in Spain, explained:

> 'People just complain about old people in the UK: "Oh, so many people getting to be retirement age; it's going to cost a lot of money in pensions and in healthcare." Whereas in Spain, you're still a very valuable member of the society. … Yes, and the social life, you get out and do things. … Spanish value older people. I think that's the difference, the Spanish do value their older people much more.'

She noted the ways in which intergenerational families interacted, for instance, when dining together in restaurants; they all helped one another. Not so, she felt, in the UK.

For the most part, US respondents in Mexico compared the ageism in their home country with the respect they experienced in Mexico. Margaret and Joseph, the 63-year-olds whom we described at the outset, voiced a common theme. Joseph spoke of how the local population just saw them as people and as members of the family who were cared for and respected. As John, who was 66, said:

> 'Young people, who I would never expect call me *caballero* ... "gentleman", they treat me with respect. They will help me in the grocery store. I mean, I don't think of myself as an old person, but sometimes, you know, it, like, takes me aback. But I can't tell you how many times people have done stuff for me. ... It's so nice.'

In the US, he said, "You feel like, 'Oh, you're, kind of, a has-been.'"

Like many of the retirement migrants, Gregory ascribed the differences between the US and Mexico as based on culture, depicting it in rather bald terms. Noting that "Old people are a little more respected here than they are in the States", he contrasted the attitudes of the latter with the former: "Old people: 'Get out of the way'" versus "Old people: 'Oh yes, you go first.'"

The experiences of 80-year-olds Martha and Leo, citizens of the US who had been in Mexico for four years, echo many of these themes. They described the way they were treated in a favourite local restaurant and how valued it made them feel. Leo said that if there was a line waiting to get in, they would be accommodated first. Martha added: "If he has troubles, they help him out. They help him to the car. They do everything they can." Above all, they felt as if they were treated as respected family members, including by the waitstaff:

> 'Every time I go in there, the maître d' and the owner (if he's here) greet me like I was the Taj Mahal queen. I'm not kidding. They come up to me. They say, "Hi, mama. How are you tonight?" They give me a hug. I can't get over it. I've never had anybody do that to me anywhere, for any reason. So, it just amazes me. ... It just overpowers me because it's never been something I've ever experienced before. ... If [the owner is] there, he greets us very lovingly and everything. But you find all these little regular servicing people who don't know us from Adam, and they're doing the same thing. ... They give us the greeting as, "Mama" and "Papa".'

Gender and visibility

Women and men spoke of their feelings of both social inclusion and freedom in their host countries differently. In his study of retirement migrants in Ecuador, Hayes (2018a) argues that women who relocated on their own felt fewer gendered constraints, and we found the same. Men and women alike mentioned the advantages of their migration discussed earlier, but women also discussed their ability to occupy space in a way that men did not. Some women spoke of their feelings of greater safety in the host country, a concern that was gendered. In some of these areas, such as Mexico, the possibility of crime drove many of our respondents into gated communities, though the gates were often more for appearance than for impregnability. Also, James reported that although neither he nor his wife had been victimised, the possibility of being robbed worried him. Still, women expressed concerns for safety *as women*. Gender inequalities mean not only that younger women's bodies are on display but also that they must be aware of the possibility of harassment or assault. In this sense, they are constrained; they lack freedom of movement. In later life, however, ageism can intersect with gender to render older women invisible; as Margaret experienced, they are often not seen (Calasanti, 2016). Although this may relieve them of being objects of harassment, they are also excluded from social life. In some ways, they do not seem to matter.

By contrast, migration brought some of the women a new sense of visibility and inclusion. Several mentioned having experienced verbal or physical harassment in their home countries – typically insults related to being both women and older. In their new countries, they felt that they could move safely in public, men were more respectful towards older women and people were less aggressive towards women than at home. Further, in some instances, they commanded better treatment as *older* women – it was an asset to be *visible* as an older woman. This sentiment was especially important for single women. Stella, a US woman in Costa Rica, provides an interesting example of this:

> 'I am a single woman. I go out and I socialise, but I don't have a car, so I walk everywhere, and even if it's night-time, I still feel very safe. I don't worry about being attacked or harassed or anything. A couple of weeks ago, I was walking from downtown to my house and there were young boys, young 12- or 13-year-old boys, and they were, like, "*Hey, chica, chica*", which means "young lady". And then I turned around and I said, "*No, soy senora*", meaning "I'm a woman". And he said, "*Oh, lo siento*", which is "I'm sorry", and then he asked me for my money, "*dinero*", and I said, "No, go away". And it was funny because he was trying to maybe flatter me by calling me "*chica*", but then he was also respectful because he changed his tune. He changed the way he approached me, and I didn't feel, like, threatened or unsafe or anything like that.'

Perhaps what is most telling in this story is that she needed to explain why she did not feel threatened by 12- or 13-year-old boys. The implication is that in her home country, she would have felt threatened, despite being an adult. She need not worry about this in her new location. Further, she felt neither invisible nor too visible; rather, she felt free. Likewise, Nina, a British woman in Spain, said:

> 'I think I feel safer. We go to Madrid quite regularly, and I'm, I may be naive, but I'm happy to walk around the streets of Madrid at night. I'm not happy to walk around the streets of London at night. It's, it's quite dangerous, or it feels frightening in the UK.'

In Mexico, Helen (aged 76) contrasted the invisibility she felt in the US with the positive kind of visibility she experienced in Mexico:

> 'You can go down the street in the United States and people will not look at you and say "Hello". ... Here, I can never go any place without every workman by the side of the road, anybody I'm walking by – I was in [nearby town] Wednesday walking, and everybody, wherever you go, everybody – You are definitely – They look at you and greet you. So ... down here, all the older people I see are out and about listening to the music – live music, dancing, interacting with each other. ... They mix. There's an awful lot of mixing of ages in the ... local venues.'

Being seen by workmen in Mexico meant being greeted, not harassed; visibility meant inclusion.

For these women, feeling socially included entailed having more control over the way they meet family demands: how much time they spent caring for others; whether they accomplish the care at some distance from families; or whether they can pass on this labour to others. It also meant moving freely in public. The extent to which this latter difference reflected their status as migrants and not locals is not clear. However, there is no doubting that this was a gendered concern.

Feeling more respected and supported provided retirement migrants with more latitude in how they felt they could behave. This added to the larger range of choices that living abroad allowed them, thanks to the greater economic security that they had in the host country compared to their home nation. This greater freedom also resulted from the diverse opportunities that our interviewees had to participate in, and contribute to, the social life of the community, as we discuss in the following.

Contributing to the local economy

The local culture was not the only reason why our interviewees felt more welcome in the host country than at home. In many respects, their value was literal: they found that their economic capital had an influence on these positive and seemingly non-ageist perceptions. In contrast to their home countries, where policy makers and others were concerned about the 'ageing population' and often presented older people as problems for the welfare state, the labour market and broader society, host countries often courted retirement migrants. For instance, in his study of lifestyle migrants, Hayes (2018a) discovered that Ecuador not only promoted some locales as ideal places for them to settle but also offered services to help integrate retirees into these areas. Similarly depicted as assets to the local economy and government, our respondents found that many local businesses – such as cafes, cultural and sports businesses, and housing and building companies – benefited from the presence of retirement migrants as consumers; indeed, some sprang up specifically to serve this population. They were thus aware that they might not survive if the latter returned to their home countries. As Jeremy (aged 63, US) explained: "[In Costa Rica, older people are treated well] by people, but the government needs dollars – that's why they've set up this immigration system that favours retirees coming and staying for long periods of time. They definitely like US retirees because that's one of their key sources of foreign currency."

David also found that retirement migrants were seen as an advantage to the local economy in Costa Rica, not only because they are consuming, "but we're also using the local labour force to help us build things, and things like that. So, I'm sure it helps [the local economy]." Indeed, the idea that retirement migrants could contribute jobs for the local population was widespread, and not just in the formal sector of the economy. In informal conversations with retired migrants in Mexico, more than one person spoke of the importance of 'hiring a staff' – someone to clean one's house, another person to garden and so on – as not only helping the retirement migrants but also a way to help those in the broader community. We will return to this topic in Chapter 6, when we examine the role of global relations more closely.

In Spain, Dan and Irène, a 66- and 58-year-old Swiss couple, had a similar impression about the advantages that retirement migrants brought to the local economy and how this engendered a status of being valued citizens, as opposed to views in their home country. Noting that he believed that these retirees "make the region run", Dan added that, as a result, the local population "must take care of pensioners". Expanding on this, Irène noted:

> 'Generally, each region which has [retirement migrants] are countries … with financial difficulties. I think that for them, the retirees are a blessing. … So, they are important to take care of. … Whereas in Switzerland, when you are retired, you don't work anymore, so you don't have any money, so, yes, I think it's different.'

The value that retirement migrants gained through their contributions to the local economy combined with the greater financial means that they attained in relocating to enhance our interviewees' feeling that they could make more decisions about how they wanted to live. This was also reinforced by the opportunity interviewees had to contribute to the local community itself.

Contributing to the local community

Volunteer activities have been widely recognised for their economic impact (Strauss, 2021). Interviewees also mentioned their volunteer activities in the local areas of their host countries as examples of how they contribute to the local communities and were valued by the local populations. Many spoke of their charitable work and cultural activities, aimed at benefitting their new regions. In Costa Rica, Josey said:

> 'Most [retirement migrants] here try to find something to do. At first, I was tutoring some girls, and then, now, tomorrow, I'm starting up with the one at the monkey rescue because they just got new babies! And so, they need people to hold them. So, I'm going to go into that a few mornings a week. So, everybody volunteers; it's such a volunteer area because nothing gets paid over here, obviously, right? Even my [US retired] neighbour is a volunteer firefighter, a "*bombero*". They don't get paid. You know. So, he's often called up, you know, to help to get a snake out of somewhere, or there's a fire over here. During the season where there are fires, they get called quite often. We help at the food bank, so we – all the girls that I know – we all go on Saturday morning once a month and go help at the food bank. ... So, there's a lot of volunteering stuff around here that gives people something to do. ... It gives you kind of a purpose.'

Jenny also volunteered in her new community, giving language lessons and helping at a food bank. She found that retirement migrants were very involved due to their free time: "The people are [very] involved in activities. [They have] time ... to do volunteer work, [which is] very satisfying to me."

In Spain, retirement migrants (mostly British) managed most of the charities (primarily distributing books and clothes), and respondents mentioned these, as well as pet-care centres and language lessons (mostly in English) to Spanish people, as important venues of social participation and self-esteem for them. Reflecting this diversity, Nina, a British woman in Spain, explained:

> 'There's so much that I can do here very easily: I'm very involved in charity work, I teach English to unemployed people and I work

for a charity ... which supports families which are really struggling financially. There's so much I can do here like that, which I thoroughly enjoy, so I'm very busy as well.'

Like Nina, Nora, another British woman, volunteered in the local council of her Spanish town. She liked being involved, as she felt that her language skills enabled her to contribute to local politics and to cultural and social associations.

Many of the US retirement migrants to Mexico volunteered in education, as children from families with little money receive limited schooling. Not only have these volunteers raised money for scholarships, but they have also created a high school where there was none. They had established a food bank and worked with schools and orphanages. Others worked with a local organisation set up to speak to medical and similar emergencies. Margaret had gathered several of the women among the retirement migrants to establish what she referred to as a "feminist group ... that we want to try to create sort of a loan system for Mexican women who are looking at starting businesses". Women among our respondents described it as providing something for women who are battered or who have financial problems. According to Joan, the group wanted to help women with skills to develop those and become entrepreneurs, and as she put it, "then they have to give back". Respondents felt that their efforts were greatly appreciated. As Susan said: "As far as Mexicans accepting expats, they are very delighted with all ... the functions and charitable offerings and commitments that ... we bring to this country or this part of the world."

Although not common, a few retirement migrants were clear that they wanted to be careful, as Margaret put it, to not "do *at* the community but *with* the community". She realised that there were many organisations up and down the coast "that want to help the community a lot". However, she wanted to be sure that they "be careful not to do so much without being aware of what Mexicans want and need ... without having their voice involved". Likewise, Maggie was involved in many local volunteer activities, bringing the talents and energies of other retirement migrants into her work. She helped build a senior centre for *abuelitas* (grandmothers and other older women only, not older men) that emerged from working with older women in two neighbouring communities and their local governments. She was also involved in fund-raising to build a fire station for the volunteer firefighters at their behest. She was clear that "we need to be sensitive to what they want. Not come in as expats and tell them what we know and what could be done, and there's a lot of them [expats] down here that do that. It's ... really wrong."

Respondents also served the retirement migrant community. Swiss interviewees organised social activities, such as a club for French-speaking retirement migrants who lived nearby. Douglas, a Swiss retiree in Spain, had created a regional association for Swiss retirees. At the time of the interview, his association had existed for more than ten years and he was still holding the presidency. He felt that by doing so, he had contributed to supporting new retirement migrants' integration into the region:

> 'I have relations with the embassy, relations with the consulate, and there are 60 of us. I organise an outing three or four times a year. Soon there will be a special traditional meal. [Some Swiss retirees] participate regularly. We meet every week. It is important for them to be together; it is an important group.'

The organisations and charities were often organised by retirement migrants themselves and did not manifest high levels of formalisation, as compared to their home countries, where organisations are increasingly formal (Alexander and Fernandez, 2021). Our interviewees felt free about how and when they wanted to contribute in their new locales, and they did not question their competence or the value of their skills for their volunteer activities. They felt that their unpaid labour made important contributions and made a positive difference in their new communities.

A community of 'alikes': being 'normal'

Living among other older people, retirement migrants also enhanced their range of choices and sense of belonging. In Spain, Nina explained that she liked living among peers who shared interests and a similar daily rhythm:

> 'You see, [this town] has so many retirees because it's obviously a place that people choose. It's, yes, it's a very comfortable life as a retiree here; there's so much here that you can do and organisations like the … University of the Third Age, which is … a great way to meet people and take up different activities. … I think that it's probably easier to be, to have a good social life here as retiree. … Over here, you're 70, the weather's nice, you go out, take a walk. Here, they organise so many things … trips and meals, and the social centre over there, they have all sorts of things going on, dances, you know.'

In Costa Rica, Joseph liked living among other retirement migrants "because they are in the same situation as us. Maybe because it's not, like, we're just the only ones, that there's other people like us." Luke and Beatrice felt that living among other retirement migrants like themselves offered them several benefits, as Luke expressed:

'Well, it's an advantage to [live among] expats. You have a choice to rather hang out with the locals, and you have a choice to hang out with a culture that you're more familiar with, people you can relate to. You can share information; you're all living in a country that's not of your birth. So, you can share and support each other. It's a network. We have a lot of good friends here.'

Many retirement migrants moved to their particular communities after visiting and, as Mike noted, "found that we have a lot of common interests with the people that are here".

Their commonality went beyond being migrants, however. Although some spoke of the ageism in their home countries, their exclusion was often more subtle. Several of our interviewees noted that social life in their home country revolved around norms set by and for younger and professionally active people. As our respondents aged, they felt increasingly marginalised and stigmatised by the surrounding youth-based lifestyle. In their new countries, they liked living among other people with whom they could identify *because* of their age status, as well as because they were retirement migrants. Our interview with Waylon, a 62-year-old man in Costa Rica, illustrates the age differences he had begun to see in the US and his inability to fit in. He discussed the prospect of growing older in the US city in which he had lived and why he saw it as a problem:

'It's a very hectic, moving city. I would use the word "yuppie". Yuppies are young professionals … up-and-coming, moving up, owning the world. … And as you get older in [this city], you want to be a bit more quiet in your life, just a bit more peace, a bit more quiet.'

Internet communities can bind groups across great distance, but physical proximity, as in neighbourhoods, still fosters friendships and networks (MacPherson et al, 2001). The process begins with homogeneity, to the extent that the ability to reside in the same area is often based on class. Within those bounds, people tend to gravitate towards, and form friendships with, those most like themselves. So it is with age, which can also serve as the foundation of community (Cornwell et al, 2008; Tulin et al, 2021).

Having relocated, our interviewees were now surrounded by those more like themselves in terms of age or life stage. They appreciated living among what Waylon referred to as "alikes" – retirement migrants who shared not only a similar life pace but also cultural and social norms that some perceived as generational. As Sherry, a US migrant to Mexico, put it:

'Oh, there's always, I think, an advantage to having some kind of common background, you know, where we kind of have some common experiences, like when we were in college, whatever it was we were doing in our youth, or something comes up and we can remember where we were or what we were doing at a particular time.'

Sarah, also in Mexico, echoed this theme: "We all grew up in the same time, and we all can relate to the same music and the same things, you know, the pop cultures of our time. So, there's a certain camaraderie." To be sure, coming from the same country was important, but our interviewees stressed that having retired and being of a similar age were critical parts of what they shared.

Along these lines, several interviewees were grateful that their communities did not revolve around those who are younger. Jenny found that living among other retirement migrants in Costa Rica presented greater opportunities for her social life than in the US, where the pace of life was set by younger, employed people. Since people in her new community were retirees like her, without rigid work schedules, they could spend time together: "You have more time for the human side of life; you can sit and have a coffee and have a conversation for an hour, with no stress or worry, or have to be in a hurry to go back to work." Some also expressed the belief that the region in which they lived in the host country was tailored more towards older, rather than younger, expatriates, whom they believed would not find jobs, friends or satisfactory occupations. For instance, talking about her area in Costa Rica, Beatrice explained: "This area isn't for young people; it's for elderly people, retired people. There's nothing for young people to do here, even for the young people who live here." This observation contrasted with interviewees' experiences of living in the more youth-based context of their home countries. In their new location, older people's culture and needs dictated much of the community structure and daily life.

Thanks to their common ages and life stages, retirement migrants felt that they could rely on their community more than in their home countries, without it being perceived by others as a problem or a sign of dependence and failed ageing. In fact, helping each other was perceived as needed to face the challenges of living abroad. Joseph explained that living among other migrants who shared similar experiences made him feel a part of a community with people upon whom he could rely for a range of reasons. Talking about his US neighbours in Costa Rica, he said:

> 'Everyone helps each other out. We don't have a car, so sometimes, they offer to give us a ride if they're going somewhere. And they have neighbourhood parties and people are at each other's house to make sure their house is safe when they're gone. So, it's nice to have neighbours, friendly neighbours, around. … Because they are in the

same situation as us. Maybe because it's not like we're just the only ones, that there's other people like us.'

In Spain, Alma indicated that, in contrast to the UK, she and her husband felt part of an international community of similar people upon whom they could rely:

'Our neighbours are French, we meet with them a lot, and the other neighbours. ... I've got no family that will help me at all. So, that's a worry: what will happen when we get very old and there's nobody. But in an international community like this, we do tend to look after one another, and help one another, more than we would back home. At home, no one really speaks to you, do they? Everybody's got their own little lives; they go back into their box at night and then they go out to work. In England ... I wonder how, if anything happened to Ivan, how I would cope.'

The ability to feel as if you can rely upon others was expressed throughout our interviews but, again, took on a particular meaning for those who were single, especially women. Stella felt secure living among other migrants from whom she could both ask for and provide support to. In the US, she said, "I didn't know my neighbours – everybody's cut off and protected from each other." By contrast, she said that in Costa Rica:

'I can call people up and say that I need help or, "Let's go out for dinner", or "Let's go and listen to this music", or whatever. And it's just very comfortable and very relaxed. I've found the community here so supportive and kind. ... Everybody is so kind and so helpful. I dog-sit. I love dogs, and so people will go home, and so I go and stay in their house and watch their animals. So, it's like a big family. That's one of the advantages ... of this town. I'm sure there are little enclaves across the country that have something similar, but this town really seems to have something special, really special.'

Helen also made clear that living among retirees in Mexico had important advantages for socialising, as a 76-year-old single woman, and to help one another:

'[Here], people are retired and they're out and about looking out for each other. ... And helping each other out I think is very nice. That I can go out and see friendly faces, talk to people. I just met another woman yesterday who's also retired and down here, and she had been at the gym but I'd talked to her at the cafe. So, I think a lot of the retirees are out and about. ... And they're friendly and so it's nice to have an encounter with them. And, you know, I think they're watching, looking out for each other. I know my neighbour, when she broke her leg ... everybody was, you know, helping her out, so it seems like a community where people seem to care about each other and to look out for each other.'

Not all interviewees felt as much a part of the community, however. Some lived in neighbourhoods mostly occupied by part-time residents, which reduced their sense of belonging. In Spain, Nina moved out of her house within such an area five years after our first interview to live in an apartment in the centre of her town, where she could socialise more frequently. In Mexico, Vera was integrated into her "Mexico family", a group of permanent residents who gathered frequently to share advice and just socialise. They all knew and cared for one another, such that when Vera brought a man who suffered from dementia to their gatherings, she did not worry about him wandering off because she knew others would pay attention. At the same time, when asked about living among retirees, Vera said that she did not have any retired neighbours; those people who owned homes on her street were all part-timers who only came on some weekends. Indeed, her street looked both well-cared-for and unused: no cars or trash cans appeared on the street. Likewise, Joan and Carl from the US felt somewhat isolated, as they also lived further than most from the main group of migrants in a neighbourhood of part-timers. Referring to it as a "bedroom community", Carl complained that they never knew when their neighbours would be coming and going, as they had other homes. As a result, and despite the fact that they loved their house, Joan and Carl voiced regret that they had been unable to find a similar house in a neighbourhood of full-timers and said that they did not feel as much a part of the retirement migrant community as they would like.

Conversely, being tight-knit can have its own downside. Margaret and Joseph, the couple mentioned at the outset of this chapter, noted that although there was a good community in Mexico, with "a lot of common values", it could be a bit too close. As Mary said, "We know each other's business a little too much, you know?" Vera reported that a woman who was a central organiser of the Mexico family gatherings had a rule that if anyone brought a date, that person was strictly "off limits" to anyone else later. Vera said that this woman believed that it would "cause friction" in the group, but her rule had "alienated" people a couple of times.

Finally, our re-interviews with a handful of retirement migrants reinforced the bases of community that they had experienced. Some interviewees' feeling of community had changed over the couple of years since we first spoke. Nora enjoyed living among other British retirement migrants in

Spain; yet, after a couple of years, she did not feel like part of the community anymore: "I found myself more isolated ... from the British people that live here", she explained, stressing that she did not share similar interests with the community of retirement migrants anymore. She mentioned a literature festival that she used to organise for her British peers but that had now disappeared. She perceived this change as resulting from politics in the UK (particularly Brexit), which polarised British migrants living in her area. Diana, whom we first interviewed in Costa Rica, had experienced a similar transformation in terms of her relationship with the community. While she first felt very included in her new country because she lived among other "white-haired people", this had changed after a "real influx" of younger people had come to live in her town within a year, making her feel less comfortable: "I just don't feel at home with them so much now", she said. In addition to stressing the importance of similar interests in constructing a feeling of inclusion, Diana's comments pointed to the importance of being surrounded by others of a similar age for those whose age would otherwise marginalise them.

Still at risk

In many respects, as we have shown, sharing age-based interests and experiences provides a sense of belonging. When age also places one in a marginal group, then being with others of similar age can also provide safe haven, or a space where one falls again within the norm. Joan speaks of her normalcy in an age-based setting. Describing where she had lived prior to her move to Mexico, she says: "We had friends who are retired up there, in our community. Our lake community was pretty close-knit. ... That community ... was very special ... it was kind of like here [Mexico]." She contrasts this to the city she and her husband had considered moving to on the West Coast of the US, where she said she saw more ageism than she did in either her former home or in Mexico. Living in a community with others of a similar age shielded Joan and her husband from exclusion.

When you are a part of the norm, or the standard, you are neither visible and deviant nor invisible. You do not stand out and are not made aware of your difference, your 'otherness'. In Mexico, James lives in a neighbourhood that was central to the retirement migrant community. His comments illustrate the normalcy fostered by this age-segregated setting:

> 'I'm 75, as you know, and I joined a gym. ... I've never gone to a gym in my life. So, here I am getting in, getting into better shape that I've probably ever been in at 75. But I never think about my age. You know, everybody around here is in a similar age range bracket. ... Sometimes, I think I'm, like, you know, 30 something.'

Residence in a community of peers helps members of marginal groups avoid exclusion. It helps both to avoid people who might exclude them and to make members normal. In this way, living among other retirement migrants, as well as feeling valued by the local communities, helped our respondents reduce social precarity and ageism.

This solution was imperfect, however. As research has shown (Levy, 2001), growing up in the ageist cultures of the Global North typically means internalising scorn for old people. Thus, respondents voiced ageism of their own as they discussed either life among other retirees or those aspects of their migration that they found problematic. They wanted to live near other retirees, but they wanted to avoid feeling surrounded by nothing but old people.

When Joan and Carl moved to Mexico, they sought more than a cheaper place with good weather and fewer allergens in the air. They rented a house in the area for a few months to see what the people around them were like, and Joan said that this helped to convince them that the location would work: "We didn't want to live in Florida with just old people [laughs], so we liked the idea of more families [who lived in the rental neighbourhood] and that sort of thing." Likewise, Meredith, herself 71 years old, spoke of the possible negatives of living in a community of retirement migrants:

> 'A bunch of old people, kind of, can drag you down where there's nothing but old people. You know, it's like, "Oh, God. Here come all those old people again." So, luckily, we've got some young people here too – young people with kids. ... So, you don't feel totally surrounded by old people.'

Mike also pointed to the benefits of youth:

> 'The disadvantage [of living here] could be that our community is older and you don't have the stimulation of younger generations, [who] have a different thought process than what we might have. You know, living in [our previous city], a very diverse community as far as demographics and age group ... even though the community that we hung with were probably closer to our age (Susan's and mine).'

On the one hand, Mike wanted more youth as a form of "stimulation". On the other hand, even when he had lived near young people, he tended to interact with those most like them in age.

We see ageism at issue here, not merely because residents call for more younger people in the communities, but rather for the reasons underlying this call and how they frame old people. These comments denigrate old people, though some of them do it implicitly. Joan and Meredith, both in their early 70s, were upfront about not wanting to be only with "old people"; other respondents likewise decried that possibility. In some respects, their comments echoed previous findings concerning older adults wanting to limit time spent in the exclusive company of old people, in part, to avoid the stigma attached to this time of life (Hurd, 1999). They may accept their chronological age but will not identify themselves as 'old' (Minichiello et al, 2000; Townsend et al, 2006), and most do this by calling for frequent interaction with, or at least proximity to, young people. Mike's reference to stimulation cites the shortcomings of other old people like himself. His implicit critique of being with others like himself implies a devaluation of them.

This call for young people to reduce the percentage of old people in retirement communities reflects ageism. It is an example of members of a marginalised group trying to align more closely with the group that enjoys greater status. Other age-homogeneous groups make no such demands: younger people do not harp on about the need to be around old people in order to raise the status of their friendship circles. The concerns of these retirement migrants reflect a popular culture message: that older people are acceptable to the extent that they are not different from younger people; and that they need to be 'young at heart' and can stay that way by interacting with youth. This is analogous to saying that marginalised ethnic groups are acceptable to the extent that they behave more like white people or at least mix with them well, or that women can be successful in the workplace the more they act like men and fit in with the boys. We do not hear this lament from those with privilege; it remains a call by marginal groups to elevate their status by association.

As we noted in Chapter 2, much has been written about retirement migrants as lifestyle migrants who follow their bliss and seek adventure. Some, like Hayes (2018a), frame this as people engaging in successful or active ageing. As depicted in popular culture, such as in the 2012 movie *The Best Exotic Marigold Hotel*, the goal of these older people is to seek adventure, empowerment and inexpensive care, often in exotic places, as a way to age well (Ciafone, 2017; Hayes, 2018a). Certainly, there were a small number of respondents in our study that talked about migrating as an adventure. Mike is one example:

> 'So, I've always been comfortable with, kind of, looking forward to new adventures and new challenges, not only personally but professionally. So … we've spent our last 19 years in [city], and I just never really felt like that was going to be part of my DNA, to live in one place for a long period of time. While it was a great experience, loved all of that time, I just felt like, for me and for us, a new adventure was something that was going to be important at that next stage of life. … [Continuing

to live there] wasn't as much for me as far as adventure. ... [F]or me, from an emotional and growth standpoint, and fulfilling that sense of adventure, that was certainly [the] number one [reason we migrated].'

Mike's comments suggest that he views later life as a time where growth would be difficult to achieve without effort, or a new adventure. In making their decision to move, Carl said that they too wondered: "Do we have another adventure in us?"

The fact of retirement migrants' search for adventure does nothing to rule out the possibility that they flee social exclusion. We suggest that scholars have not critically examined the notion of lifestyle migration in relation to age relations and thus miss the dimension of ageism that can drive it. To be sure, the sense of migration as adventure, rather than a means of survival, may be more prevalent among retirees with greater financial wherewithal. (However, as we have argued, those with low incomes can and do see their relocation as providing them greater freedom.) Still, neither the quest for adventure nor their efforts to survive financially negate the social precarity shared by our respondents. The spectre of becoming 'old' and marginalised as such was an ever-present risk they faced.

Conclusion

Our interviews and fieldwork revealed a form of social precarity (which we defined as the risk of social exclusion) that has been little explored in relation to retirement migration. This social precarity stems from ageism and affects all older people, not only those with lower incomes; we found that retirement migrants feel more socially included in their host countries than in their home countries irrespective of their economic status.

Some feelings arose when their advanced age rendered them a distinct group and seemed to shape their treatment. Our interviewees reported, first, that older people garnered more respect and deference in Spanish, Costa Rican and Mexican cultures, and that this made them feel more valuable. They found that those communities accepted them as they were and appreciated their presence, whereas their home countries perceived older people as a problem: dependants that burdened their families, economies and states. A gender dimension emerged as well, wherein women expressed a particular freedom: that of being able to be visible and safe. They felt neither invisibility nor harassment.

Second, retirement migrants believed that they were welcome in the host countries because they contributed to community well-being. They felt that their greater economic power relative to the local populations gave them the ability to fuel the economies and that they were assets to local businesses and governments. They also saw the local communities as benefitting from the retirement migrants' volunteer and charitable work, and this added to their sense of being welcomed, rather than excluded. Organising support, either formally or informally, for other migrants also made retirement migrants feel that they were contributors, rather than burdens.

Retirement migrants' feelings of inclusion owed to surrounding themselves with others much like them: migrants in the second part of their life course. This helped them to develop a sense of belonging and support, and contrasted with the prospect of isolation that they had left behind in their home countries, where finding supportive and inclusive communities for older people was thought to be difficult. In their new locales, much of social life revolved around older people's interests and schedules; this differed from their home countries, which they saw as based more on young people's lives and pace. Rather than being excluded because they were older, they formed bonds that related to their ages. As a result, they felt freer in their host countries, while at home, they had felt deviant and more constrained.

We also found that although migration can allow these older people to find support among like-minded peers, this does not challenge ageism; rather, it merely forestalls the social precarity. Interviewees indicated that they had grown up with ageism and had internalised it. As a result, some of them reproduced ageism as they spoke to us. For instance, many spoke of the high proportion of older people as a *dis*advantage of where they lived. They did not challenge the negative views concerning old age but instead sought to avoid being seen as members of an old folk's community. Therefore, although the migration reduced their social precarity, it did not eliminate it entirely. We anticipate that they will face more of it as they age.

Retirement migration can help older people escape the age-based social precarity in their home countries and the depictions of older people as problems, or as burdens. In their host countries, they feel accepted, both interpersonally and by the broader society, and freer to decide how to live their lives. This integration is imperfect; previous research shows that some retirement migrants occupy a liminal space, where are welcomed but still retain distance from the local population (O'Reilly, 2000), a topic to which we return in Chapter 6. In terms of their own communities, as we have shown, retirees' own ageism can also preclude connections among their peers; past studies make clear that retirees' communities can also foster exclusion through gossip and other means of social control (Oliver, 2007, 2008). Finally, we do not argue that the host countries are not ageist (or are less ageist). Nor do we assert that our respondents are wrong in saying that their new communities are without ageism. The economic and social advantages that retirement migrants find abroad rely on a global system of inequalities, in which richer countries and their citizens dominate poorer ones. What our interviewees ascribed to cultures that respect older people and lack ageism might result more from migrants' power based in the Global North. The deference they received as older people is not easily disentangled from that obtained as a result of the global inequalities that drive their migration. We address this in Chapter 6, contextualising retirement migration within global power relations.

6

Relying on global privileges

Introduction

Sherry (age 70) and her husband Gregory (age 71) have lived in Mexico for a few years. They have been married for 30 years; each had been married once previously. Sherry has two children from her previous marriage; she and Gregory did not have any children together. Sherry is close to her daughter, who is moving for a new job that will also make it easier for her to see her mother in Mexico, and she will see her more often. Sherry is less close to her son, though they speak about once a month; she says that he will never visit. She is not close to her step-grandchildren, all of whom are grown.

When Gregory retired, Sherry was still employed and could work remotely if need be. If she could afford it, she would have preferred to move back to a city where she had once lived on the East Coast of the US, but that was too expensive. They looked at some places in Mexico, spending a couple of months in each, and did the same in some cities in the US. Eventually, they rented a place in Mexico, with the thought of staying for two years to see whether it facilitated being close enough to their daughter and son-in-law. They decided that it would work for them, both for family and for health reasons. Both Sherry and Greg had multiple chronic health issues. They maintained their healthcare providers in the US and held open the possibility that, as they aged, they would establish relationships with healthcare practitioners in Mexico.

The combination of their ability to see her daughter and son-in-law, access to desired healthcare, and economic considerations swayed them towards Mexico. As they were fairly well off, their economic reasoning bore more explanation:

'So, in 2015, we were down [here] … and the peso was trading at about one to 12. At the end of year, we came down and we actually took a trip. We drove from [US state] to here and then drove down to Baja Peninsula, took the ferry over to the mainland and then went on up to Lake Chapala. The peso was just creeping up at that point; it went to 14. It was like, "Oh, my gosh. What a windfall it is." Well, you know, now is hovering around 20. So, certainly for us, that's an advantage. It breaks my heart for locals and what it's meaning for them, but certainly that has created an opportunity for us. The opportunity is that we can live on our Social Security without … touching our portfolio. So, thinking of this strategically, it makes a lot of sense to do that. ... I understand that people spend on average 85 per cent of what they'll spend in healthcare, they'll spend in the last two years of their lives. So, we don't want to deplete all of our assets and then need something, care facility or treatments. So, economics has been part of it. You know, saying that, I mean, we could achieve the same economic benefits being ... anyplace else in Mexico, of course. ... [But] we have been able to build a wonderful community here, meet people who have similar values and enjoy their company, develop nice relationships. So, it feels very comfortable.'

Maggie's migration story differs in many ways from that of Sherry and Gregory. As a divorcee, she had been married for only a short time. She has two daughters and grandchildren, with whom she is close. They resisted her move so far from them, and not specifically for wanting her to care for the grandchildren (Maggie said that she did not do that and emphasised at many points in the interview that she was very independent). Her kids wanted Maggie available to them, just to be around.

A self-described free thinker who lived near the ocean in different US states for almost 40 years, including a move to be closer to her children during the previous period of time, Maggie has lived in Mexico for just over a year. She retired at 65, when she understood (somewhat mistakenly) that she was "fully vested" in SS.[1] She had been self-employed for most of her career but had worked for a large corporation over the last seven years, which she did not enjoy much. She retired when she felt "ready for my next big adventure".

Despite having worked for so many years, however, Maggie's SS benefits were only about USD 1,100 a month; she could not have afforded to retire where she had been living in the US. At the time of our interview, she supplemented her benefits with small, part-time jobs. She worked intermittently for a company related to her previous employment in the US; it paid well, but it was a rarity. Her other part-time work gained her about USD 360 a month. Her financial situation was indeed precarious.

Beyond her meagre pension, Maggie had no savings or other sources of income. She owned her small house in Mexico but leased the land. Had she stayed in the US, she would likely qualify for Medicaid (healthcare for those in poverty) in her home state. Indeed, she saw this as her possible future. She did not otherwise wish to return to the US but saw that she might need to do so for medical care. Otherwise, she preferred to remain in Mexico. Since she lived alone, she felt it important to pay USD 20 a year for an emergency medical service that would provide an ambulance. She also continued to pay premiums for Medicare on the chance that she would return to the US for necessary medical care.

Sherry, her husband, and Maggie are in the same general location in Mexico, with two contrasting stories of how and why they moved there. Both were economically motivated, but Sherry and Greg could live well "without touching their portfolio", whereas Maggie's economic situation was precarious. She was able to survive financially only because of her extra income from part-time jobs.

Despite these difference in financial security, a common thread binds them: global inequalities that give them pathways to services that they might not otherwise afford. In this chapter, we will examine how global relations influenced our retirement migrants' abilities to improve their lives across the three countries. In Chapter 7, we look at healthcare and personal assistance in the same terms, that is, as shaped by relations between home nations, which have become too expensive for many people to live in, and the host nations to which retirees migrate.

Precarity and privilege

In the previous chapters, we discussed the interplay of financial and social precarities in retirement migration contexts. Austerity welfare state policies and other features of neoliberalism, such as major financial crises and highly competitive labour markets, have shaped many of our participants' life courses and financial well-being. For instance, we saw in Chapter 4 that some retirement migrants, especially women, had experienced precarity both because of their low-paid and insecure jobs, and because of welfare state policies that kept pension benefits and, in some countries, health insurance coverage too low for comfort. Likewise, as documented in Chapter 3, welfare states have often fingered old people as the basis for states' fiscal situations, pointing to their dependence on pensions and need for healthcare, a depiction that contributes to ageism regardless of retirees' financial resources. In such contexts, retirement migration can increase both financial security and social inclusion. In this chapter, we illuminate the ways in which retirement migrants can be both precarious and privileged.

Transnationalism – the movement and development of social networks across national borders – is central to understanding the local and global structures of retirement migration, and it is also shaped by global inequalities. Waldinger and Fitzgerald (2004: 1177) make clear that migrants' 'connectivity between source and destination' relies not only upon their decision to relocate but also upon nation states' policies and the relationships between these nations. Further, older migrants encounter diverse and unequal constraints on their ability to move across borders (Hunter, 2018; Torres, 2019; Bolzman, 2021; Mahfoudh et al, 2021). Some, especially those from poorer countries, face an array of restrictions when they cross borders. By contrast, older migrants from richer countries of the Global North move across borders with few, if any, constraints.

Second, as previously mentioned, citizens of the Global North are not all equally able to live transnationally. Depending on their citizenship and economic statuses, retirement migrants have uneven possibilities to benefit from their retirement pensions and health insurances in the country of migration, as illustrated by different scholars (Gehring, 2017; Kosnick et al, 2021). Along these lines, we saw in Chapter 4 that the retirement migrants in our study faced different constraints based on their citizenship.

Finally, research by such authors as Benson (2013, 2015), Hayes (2015, 2018a, 2018b) and Miles (2015) highlights how North–South migrants make use of global power relations rooted in postcolonial structures to bolster their socio-economic status at the expense of the local population. Retirement migrants draw upon these global inequalities to obtain inexpensive living conditions and higher social status, even when such movement occurs in countries 'that were not directly colonised' (Benson, 2015: 21). These authors find that North–South migrants' lifestyles and self-perceptions reflect their advantages, typically as they exoticise the local population, take for granted their privileges over the latter, underpay them for their services and acquire land at prices that are affordable for them but inaccessible to the local population. Such global power relations are particularly visible in the global market of long-term care: older people from richer countries can draw upon their global privileges to pay cheaper and 'loving' female care workers, either in their home countries (Repetti and Schilliger, 2021) or abroad (Bender et al, 2017; Bender and Schweppe, 2022).

Drawing on these observations, we begin this chapter by showing how our interviewees' citizenship statuses allow them to move with relative ease between their home and host countries, as well as elsewhere. We then discuss the role that low-cost means of transportation and communication (such as cheap flights and Internet access) play in retirement migrants' ability to engage in 'transnational ageing' (Hunter, 2018: 197), as well as the economic, social and political uncertainties that can reduce retirement migrants' ability to travel. We highlight how global inequalities both foster and constraint opportunities for retirees from privileged countries to meet their financial, social and care needs, enabling them to achieve better socio-economic positions while residing in poorer regions of the world. Finally, we explore the tensions that emerge from the participants' experiences of migration, which reveal how local and global power relations intertwine in these contexts.

Transnationalism

Citizenship

Transnationalism is central to our interviewees' migration. International agreements and the interviewees' citizenship in countries of the Global North facilitated their migration and travel in and out of their host countries. Hayes

(2018a: 20) argues that this ease of movement from North to South reflects 'the global divisions of labor ... as individuals from former colonies occupy positions of service for individuals who, in many cases, are citizens of states that those former colonies served'. For instance, Nora, a British retiree in Spain, talked about the advantages her European citizenship afforded her, enabling her to travel and get access to healthcare abroad:

> 'I've just got from Britain my European health card. I got a new one because I'm in the Spanish health service, but I get it from Britain. And it allows me still to go to all European Union countries and Switzerland and Norway, I think, and I can use that for emergency healthcare in all those countries still.'

We should emphasise that Nora's views reflect a pre-Brexit context. Since Brexit has come into being, however, British citizens' statuses within the EU have changed, with negative consequences for their sense of freedom regarding migration and settlement (Benson et al, 2022). Swiss retirees had similar advantages as the British prior to Brexit. Thanks to the Schengen Agreement, they could travel within countries of the EU without major restrictions.

US retirees also benefited from advantages of their citizenship and international agreements, which enabled their travel and life in host countries without administrative impediments. Even some of the interviewees who did not have legal, permanent residence status in their host countries (a situation we encountered in Costa Rica and Mexico) could stay there with relatively ease with a tourist permit, while maintaining health coverage in their home countries. Justin, a 63-year-old US early retiree in Costa Rica, was a good example of this. He had not completed the process leading to a Costa Rican residence permit due to a lack of money and was not planning to. Therefore, he considered himself a 'perpetual tourist', and every 90 days, he left the country (by car) to get a new tourist visa. Justin had enough money to pay for minor health issues in Costa Rica and, as a military veteran, could use US veteran hospitals. Thus, he had a relatively secure situation: "If I go to the private doctor or something and I pay out of pocket, but if I get major surgery or injury ... I will fly to Florida and go to ... hospital. I've got it all figured out. ... I'm a perpetual tourist." Justin's situation was not unique. He stressed that there was no law in Costa Rica that prevented him from leaving the country and coming right back. He preferred to avoid becoming a permanent resident in Costa Rica, as this would require him to pay taxes that he otherwise did not have to pay.

Louis, a US retiree in Costa Rica, also had no permanent residence in Costa Rica. However, in contrast to Justin, he planned to obtain it soon. In the meantime, he was still covered by Medicaid, a means-tested health insurance plan that pays for healthcare provided in the US, and could pay out of pocket for minor healthcare issues in Costa Rica: "I have health insurance from my home state [in the] US. That means that if you don't make a certain amount of money, the state will pay for a part of your health insurance." Louis indicated that he understood that he would eventually need to use Costa Rican health insurance and drop the state Medicaid plan: "We'll see when that happens, but, yes, eventually, I will have to do that. I just don't know when that is."

Similar to coming up with ways to be perpetual tourists, some respondents in Mexico stretched the boundaries of what was allowed, often violating the spirit, if not the letter, of the law to avoid paying for car registrations or taxes in Mexico, for instance, or to maintain medical coverage in the US. As William put it, a lot of the retirement migrants knew how to work the system and were "flying under the radar". It was apparent that the advice was shared within the "Mexican family", as Vera called it. Migrants would "bounce stuff off of each other ... so no one makes the same mistakes", including knowledge of how to game the system by skirting regulations or playing national rules against one another. Some of this knowledge was key to survival for some of the US retirement migrants – in both Mexico and Costa Rica – who might otherwise struggle to obtain healthcare, for example. For others, it was simply knowledge that migrants passed on to one another concerning how to navigate life in their new country in the most beneficial way. In either case, they learned to take advantage of life in their new countries, regardless of their prior economic positions in their home nations.

International travel

The lack of administrative constraints allowed our interviewees to travel internationally on a regular basis, mostly by plane and sometimes by car. Patricia, a British woman in Spain, often travelled between Spain and the UK to see children and grandchildren: "I go [by plane] once every seven weeks, and I stay five days." This allowed her to maintain her family ties.

Many participants noted that being able to live relatively close to an airport played an important role in deciding where to migrate, as the proximity allowed for geographic flexibility and facilitated frequent travels to their home country. As Nina, a British retiree in Spain, explained:

> 'One thing ... about this town is that we have two airports and we can fly from either of them. ... And it's pretty much the same distance, only an hour and a bit both [ways], very, very easy. And our children live near an airport in the UK. And so, it's easy for us, it's very easy to fly to them.'

David, a US retiree in Costa Rica, shared similar appreciation for having two airports nearby, including one that was easily reached by car. He and his wife took this access into account when they looked for a place to settle in Costa Rica.

Migrants emphasised the importance of living a short flight time away from their home country; they typically wanted to be able to join their families within a couple of hours (preferably within two to two-and-a-half hours to airports for most European interviewees in Spain) or at a manageable drive for some. Before migrating, most of them had lived a short distance by private or public transportation (car, bus or train) from their family. For instance, Irene, a Swiss retiree in Spain, explained how she and her husband were supporting one of their children and that they looked after their grandchildren. This increased the frequency of their travel. Irene explained again how important this proximity had been in their selection of a new place to settle:

> 'And one of the reasons why we decided to relocate to Spain, rather than to a more distant country, was that it shouldn't be too far away. … Because we have our children and even our grandchildren, that it should be two hours, two hours thirty maximum. We had gone to Morocco. It was four hours from Geneva, or even elsewhere, it was a bit long. We saw that it would be a problem if [our children needed us]. And then especially Switzerland is accessible by car from Spain, so there you go.'

A few interviewees journeyed more widely. Claire, a British retiree in Spain whose family was dispersed around the world, travelled large distances to spend time with her family. She and her husband spent about eight weeks a year with family in Australia and met with family in other locations that vary from year to year.

In Mexico, some participants travelled to the US to see family, access healthcare or purchase goods and services not as easily acquired in Mexico. For instance, one couple regularly cared for a grandchild when school in the US was not in session. Crossing borders was easy for our interviewees in Mexico thanks to their US passports. This was part of their global privilege, contrasting with South – North migrants, for whom crossing such borders could present far more constraints (Gehring, 2016, 2017).

US interviewees in Costa Rica also took distance from family into account when making their migration decisions. As Kelly and her husband Jimmy noted, the primary reason they chose Costa Rica was because of its proximity to family; had they gone to Thailand, "We wouldn't see anybody." However, especially for those retirement migrants in Costa Rica, economic resources shaped their transnational movements. All were not equally able to travel across borders, as flights to the US were relatively expensive and travelling by car was not possible. Interviewees in Spain or Mexico could generally use low-cost airlines or drive to their home countries.

Moving with relative ease between countries and having access to healthcare abroad was a major aspect of many of our interviewees' experiences of retirement migration. However, their reports make clear that retirement migration sits at the juncture of local and global inequalities. Transnationalism is not as easy for all older people globally, and relying on cheap and frequent travel – particularly by plane – raises questions of the sustainability of such movement in a world increasingly shaped by global warming and resultant environmental challenges (Repetti and Lawrence, 2021). Most participants paid relatively little for travel, whether by air, train or car, and they benefited from citizenship-related advantages that were not equally accessible to local populations in the countries in which our interviewees lived. In the following, we elaborate on the intersection of global and local inequalities by exploring two key themes that emerged from our interviews: the tensions between inclusion and exploitation; and relations with the locals reflecting global structures of domination.

Local and global inequalities: taking advantage or helping the local people?

In Chapter 4, we discussed retirement migrants' experience of economic inclusion in their host countries, contrasting it with the economic precarity in their home countries, from which most had sought to escape. In Chapter 5, we showed that retirement migrants felt more included socially in their host countries, in part, because they faced less ageism there than at home. However, their testimonies also revealed exploitative colonial relations on which their inclusion depended in Spain, Costa Rica and Mexico. Those power relations shaped their perceptions of the local populations and the way in which they interacted and did business with them. The reality of these global inequalities calls into question the extent to which their perception of a lack of ageism was due to greater respect for older people or to their greater power in the colonial relation.

Inclusion through exploitation

Retirement migrants' economic inclusion – and their sense of being valued for their contributions – mostly relies upon their capacity to buy (or rent) cheaper housing, as well as other goods and services, especially healthcare, in their host countries. Their ability to do so results from the inequalities in economic power between their home and host countries (Benson, 2015; Bell, 2017; Hayes, 2018a, 2021; Rainer, 2019). Global power structures had allowed them to bolster their personal savings or benefit from the sale of property by migrating to countries where land and housing are cheaper (Rainer, 2019). Likewise, their retirement pensions, which were often relatively low in their home countries, gained more value in their host countries and reduced their financial precarity. Damian, a US retiree in Costa Rica, described his advantages:

> 'My wife [and I] made some money on the house that we sold when we came here. We don't have to worry about money until, well ... we don't really have to worry about it. Then, I'll have Social Security in a few years, and we'll just leave that money alone and have that money to travel. ... If I retired ... and stayed in the United States, I couldn't afford it. I would be out of money in 10–15 years. ... [But] we can live down here for less than USD 2,000 a month. ... That includes health insurance, food, everything.'

The lower cost of living resulting from global inequalities also means that retirement migrants have more disposable income, which they can use to hire local workers. In this sense, even those retired migrants who would otherwise be economically precarious could have more economic power than the local population. Their relative deprivation in the Global North became relative power in the South. Migrants also pointed to the expectation that they would contribute to the local communities by hiring people to cook, to garden or to clean for them. At a local gathering that the second author attended in Mexico, a migrant told her: "You should have staff. ... It helps you, and it also helps them. They need the money, and it is better to have them work and get paid."

At the same time, respondents spoke of a 'balance' they felt they should maintain to sustain the larger inequality. They believed that they should pay local workers well, though not so much that they would be out of line with the local economies, and ensure that the workers are worth what they are receiving. Meredith exemplifies this ethos. Living comfortably in Mexico, she knew she had far more income than others in her community; she was aware of her privilege in that regard but wanted to be careful. As she put it: "I try to do good things with the resources that I have but not something where I feel like I'm being taken advantage of, you know." Such beliefs undergird retirement migrants' ability to view their transnational movement as 'unproblematic and often even helpful to the local community' (Hayes, 2018a: 59), even as they pay very low wages for personal service.

In contrast, older local people in host countries did not have the ability to increase the value of their economic resources by relocating abroad, something that our interviewees rarely mentioned. Respondents spoke little about either the inequality between them and the local populations, or their exploitation of local people, energy and land. The contrasting stories that opened this chapter demonstrate the differences among our interviewees' understandings. Sherry noted the discrepancies in wealth that accrue to global relations and the peso's decline relative to the US dollar. Although she said, "It breaks my heart for the locals", she focused on the "opportunities" it created for her and her husband, and the fact that, as a result, they could live well "without even touching our portfolio". Implicitly, she acknowledged that she was benefitting at the expense of the local population.

Few retirement migrants seemed to question how their status in their new countries related to the disadvantaged positions of those in their host countries. Only Maggie showed concern for this, complaining that her fellow migrants were "taking advantage in many ways of the cheapness down here and the beauty [of the landscape], without really understanding or getting to know the people". This is not to say that the retirement migrants were blind to their privileges in their new countries; however, for the most part, they seemed content with it. At the very least, they saw it as beyond their control and were grateful for their position. As Hayes (2018a) found among retirement migrants in Ecuador, our interviewees' focus on their own household finances obfuscated larger global relations.

Meredith, mentioned earlier as one of those who believed it important to hire local workers, provides an example of how migrants often came to justify their present situations. She had lived in Mexico for 15 years and lived alone for the majority of that time. She felt that she had become a part of the local community. Meredith had many reasons to feel that she was well integrated. She explained that when she first came to Mexico, she and her husband rented a house in a different area, one that had many large homes belonging to part-timers who hired staff to keep up their houses even when they were not there. She wondered how the workers felt about this and how this would affect her relationship with the local community: "I have a hundred times more than they have as far as my resources. And I don't want to be somebody who they feel, 'Oh, she'll give me everything I want.' I don't – that's not the relationship I want with people." Meredith worried that she would be resented but then learned from conversation with one of her workers (who later became her 'Mexican family') that she need not worry. She asked him how he felt about the fact that another local group had benefits (through land rights) that he did not have. He responded: "Oh, that's just luck. You got born in the – [You are] a member of the [group] or you didn't, you know? It's not a big deal. I don't care." Commenting on this response, Meredith added: "So, it wasn't like he was resentful about, that some people had something else more than him, so." As a result, she had been able to accept the fact that, "You know, it's not really like I did anything better than anybody else; I just happened to be born who I was and I had these opportunities, and

I got this, kind of, stuff and now here I am." This had allowed her to feel "really good about my relationship with people down here, which I think is the best part about being here". She also said that she was closer to her Mexican family than to anyone else.

Like Meredith, interviewees spoke of playing vital roles in support of local communities. Several spoke with pride of their contributions (see Chapter 5). What they did not discuss were the postcolonial relations that made it easy for them to become donors to the poor people nearby. Rather, as observed by Benson (2015), they seemed to take national inequalities for granted. For example, many British and US retirees volunteered to teach English, a valuable skill in the global economy. Fluency in English for those who also mastered Spanish allowed some to attain leadership positions in local charity organisations, as Jenny, a US retiree in Costa Rica, did. At the time of her first interview in 2018, Jenny had just arrived in Costa Rica, and she was lonely. Her situation had improved by the time of the second interview in 2021. Despite the COVID-19 lockdowns that isolated many people, she felt much more included and valued than she had three years prior, the result of her having volunteered in a local food bank for a while. Since 2020, the upsurge in the local population's needs during the COVID-19 pandemic both increased her work and brought her recognition from the whole community. Her ability to take on this work was influenced by her financial resources, the ability to speak both English and Spanish fluently, and social networks in both Costa Rica and the US.

In his book on Spain, Tremlett (2006: 122) notes how migrants from the UK 'fooled themselves that they were living a Spanish lifestyle' but, after a decade, tended to remain in their British communities and still spoke few words of Spanish. In like manner but years later, we also found that most interviewees in Spain, Mexico and Costa Rica acknowledged that learning Spanish was important to understanding the people and the culture where they lived, but they had not, or they were 'planning to'. The reality was that our interviewees could get by without ever learning the language, as they mostly lived in large (sometimes gated) retirement migrant communities, and many of the locals could speak a bit of English (or French). Most of these towns also had an English-speaking market economy for the migrants, providing them with a large selection of goods and services. The advantaged position of our interviewees, especially those from the UK and US, allowed them to avoid having to master the local language; in contrast, the disadvantaged status of the locals did require them to learn some English if they wanted to participate fully in the local economy.

Privilege and views of local peoples

Our interviewees' views of the local populations in the three host countries were mostly shaped by their privileged position. Our respondents associated locals with a loving, unassuming and undemanding human nature; they usually described them as welcoming, warm-hearted and respectful in their treatment of older people. In a word, our interviewees felt that they received *deference*, the respect and esteem given to superiors. They identified these not as results of global power structures but instead as inherent in local cultures.

As other scholars of retirement migration have found (for example, Hayes, 2018a, 2018b), interviewees expressed concerns about the locals' attitudes towards them, especially related to language and money, which reinforced their outsider status. For instance, several migrants believed that local people sought to take advantage of them by raising prices when selling products to them and other expatriates, often referred to as "*gringo* pricing" or the "*gringo* tax" by migrants in Mexico and Costa Rica. Vera, a US retiree in Mexico, put it succinctly: "[T]he problem down here is, if you're Mexican, it's one price, if you're American, it's another price." This could be worrisome for those with the lowest incomes, such as Jenny, who, in her first interview, expressed concern about the higher, rising prices for consumer goods in regions in which expats lived versus the areas inhabited by locals. Similarly, Justin, a US retiree in Costa Rica, had seen healthcare prices increase, which was a concern for him, as he did not have much money:

> 'Four years ago, it was very affordable [in this area]. The more and more the *gringos* or the expats with money come here, the more the doctors will probably realise that they can charge more money for healthcare for the non-nationals. For the nationals, they charge [less], I'm not sure, because if you don't have money, doctors give you a discount for their services. Here, it's the jungle, you do what you want to do.'

Justin found that increases in the number of expatriates where he lived lead to growth of living costs, making them unaffordable for the local population. Some interviewees believed that local residents, or their culture, were to blame for their economic deprivation. This belief permeated much of the interviewees' talk about the locals, as did the belief that as retirement migrants hoping to employ locals as domestic help and volunteer with charities, they were helping to rectify this situation. As noted earlier, others might have a glimmer that the disadvantaged situation of local populations go deeper, but any analysis remains at the individual level, never touching on global financial policies, perhaps because their own personal decisions are all that they feel they can control. Meredith's discussion earlier exemplifies this latter scenario. She spoke at length about her incorporation into the community: that she was a godmother for a local child and that she had helped people who worked for her to have better lives. At the same time, she made clear that she was careful not to just give them things: that locals needed to earn them.

The mention of a '*gringo* tax' made clear that retirement migrants never felt completely included in the local populations; as William, a US retiree in Mexico, put it: "You will always be an outsider." However, many respondents knew that their valued social status as older people was owed to the economic resources that they brought with them. We showed in Chapter 5 that some interviewees felt that the retirement migrants "make the region run". They also knew that this role in the economy could work against them in relationships with locals. They accepted this, even if they were annoyed by it, as the price of living in a community that did not seem to devalue older people and that improved their economic security. While they felt that they were being exploited by the '*gringo* pricing' (see also Hayes, 2018b), they were also content to be outsiders, as they were still in an advantaged position. Reflecting this observation, Maggie, discussed earlier, overtly countered the claims made by the other respondents about how much they were a part of the local community. Summarising and contradicting the typical assertions made by other respondents, she noted that many did hire local people but that most retirement migrants were not "integrating" and maintained a distant relationship with the local population: "They have people that work for them, you know, but they're still workers for them. It's like, well, 'Do you know their family? Do you know anything about them? ... Besides giving them the extra money at Christmas that you're supposed to give them.'" Along these lines, she added: "[Retirement migrants] live in their own little bubble. But when I work with the community, there's a lot of suspicion [of expats] because [the expats] don't feel the connection ... and the curiosity, you know, about who these people [are]." Maggie's observations also put a dent in retirement migrants' claims about why they are valued and respected; as we noted, it was unclear to what extent retirement migrants' experiences resulted from less ageism, from deference born of global relations and greater economic power, or from both. The following comments by Sarah (from the US) on how she was treated by Mexicans are typical and reflect this tangle:

> 'They're very respectful, they're very nice. You know, I don't know because most of the people we've contact with are, you know, you're employing them, they're doing something for you, so they're very nice. The ... help in the store, if you go shopping, everybody's very, very nice. They treat us very nicely.'

Likewise, Carla (from the US) says of Mexicans and older people:

> 'They respect older people more than they do in the States. ... And I see that, for instance, with my workers. I feel that respect. I mean,

even though all my workers call me "Carla", I feel that respect to me as an older person, and I think that just comes from the familial society because they take care of their grandmothers.'

Sarah and others seemed vaguely aware of the way in which their economic power coloured their treatment; however, as we showed in Chapter 5, they tended to see their higher status in their new country as based on culture. By contrast, Maggie placed the blame on global relations and power:

'[Expats] are, on the surface, treated with a great deal of respect because they bring money into the community, you know? And they create jobs for everyone, you know, whether or not it's cleaning your house or working in your yard or washing your car ... cleaning your windshields. I mean, bringing food to your house. They do – [the local people are] incredibly industrious. ... But some people just use it. They just assume – What's the word? – privilege. They bring their privilege with them. ... I don't know if they really realise or care if they're respected or honestly respected or treated on equal grounds ... because they're not, you know? But the Mexicans don't feel that they are either. And so, then there's a bit of a – Fakery almost? It's not real evident, but if you ... show interest in who they are, hearts open up.'

When asked, Maggie said she learned these things from a friend who spoke fluent Spanish; from a member of the local government; and from conversations with the workers she hired. She ended by adding to her compatriots' view that the locals were likely to profit from retirement migrants. She said that their relationship with expats was "not usury, but it's like that, you know".

Thus, retirement migrants were aware of some of the ways in which economic inequalities shaped their interactions with the local population, particularly when they experienced differential treatment not to their advantage, such as having to pay higher prices for certain items. At the same time, few of them seemed aware of the possible links between global inequalities and the attention and respect that they received, and even fewer questioned this. Instead, they saw this positive treatment as a result of the culture and nature of the local population.

Conclusion

This chapter has explored how local and global power structures shape retirement migrants' inclusion in their host countries and their relationships with the local populations. First, we observed that Global North migrants could live abroad while maintaining relationships with families in their home countries or other parts of the world. Retirement migrants' transnationalism relies upon the ability to live abroad without major administrative impediments, a privilege provided by their citizenship. Their roots in a nation with significant global power shapes their migration. They can use cheap means of transportation, such as low-cost flights (see also Repetti and Lawrence, 2021) or ground transportation.

Second, the power relations between their home and host countries serve to bolster the value of migrants' financial resources and address their economic precarity. Their disposable income allows retirement migrants to hire underpaid local people, typically for domestic and outdoor labour. Their privileged global position also provides them with various ways to participate in valued roles in the host societies, and gain a sense of inclusion. They can more easily volunteer because they are fluent English speakers and draw on professional networks, allowing them to lead local charities and non-governmental organisations. Their dominant status buys them inclusion in the local communities even when they do not know the language.

Third, global domination shapes retirement migrants' perceptions of locals. Although most migrants feel included, they are more likely to count members of the expatriate communities, rather than the local populations, as peers. Reflecting Benson's (2015) observation noted earlier, retirement migrants are likely to either idealise local peoples or treat them with distrust or disregard. While migrants are aware of their economic power and the disadvantages of the locals around them, they tend to be unaware of or ignore the global power structures that create it. Even on those occasions where they evince broader understandings of the inequalities, they tend to accept them. They do not pursue any change beyond their contributions to local charities.

As we saw in Chapter 5, local populations understand that they need to be deferential to sell their products to, or gain employment from, retirement migrants. This dynamic owes not to anything that retirement migrants do but instead to a larger set of arrangements between nations. Migrants partake of those relations even if unaware of them. They know about the *gringo* tax, and locals, in turn, know to show deference. Ultimately, retirement migrants' belief that older people like themselves are more valued in their new countries – that these cultures are less ageist – cannot be disentangled from their relative economic power and global privilege. As we will see in Chapter 7, a similar dynamic enhances their healthcare and assistance with daily life. The satisfaction that they take in the care they receive is as likely tied to their economic power as to any reverential culture in their host countries.

7

Health and assistance precarity in later life

Introduction

A recognition of precarity in the lives of older people appears in the recent move among International Living media outlets to advertise not just lifestyle and leisure but retirement migration 'as a pathway to security in a volatile world' (Croucher, 2022: 175). Here, marketers refer to more than financial security; they report that, after affordability, healthcare is now the most important factor that retirees consider when they think about whether and where to migrate. This concern is perhaps especially salient for older people from the US, where healthcare can be costly, who comprise the bulk of International Living media consumers (Croucher, 2022). However, as we will show, retirement migrants across the three countries we examine worry about these issues.

Often subsumed under the rubric of healthcare is the need for daily assistance that can occur in later life even among people with no immediate need of medical care. Although such support for daily living can be tied to health, it can result from changes in abilities, such as a decline in eyesight. Assistance with ADLs or IADLs differs from healthcare and is defined as separate from healthcare in such countries as the UK, where so-called 'medical' and 'non-medical help' are referred to as 'medical care' and 'social care', respectively (Simmonds, 2021). Each of these can present distinct challenges in later life.

In terms of healthcare, both writers for media outlets and personal testimonials bear witness to the accessibility and quality of care in such countries as Costa Rica, Spain and Mexico, which were ranked the first, second and fourth best countries, respectively, for healthcare by International Living (2021). The differences in costs between the home countries of our respondents and these destinations cannot be denied. However, the quality of care is also promoted as superior (Croucher, 2022). One author compares the US and Mexico as follows: 'The primary difference ... is that the care system [in Mexico] is not profit driven. Decisions for your care and well-being are not filtered through or guided by any profit motive. Doctors take plenty of time with you and a large number still perform house visits for patients' (Murray, 2022: 1). That healthcare should be an important issue for older people is not surprising; however, as the previous quote suggests, at issue is not only the availability but also the quality of healthcare. This latter notion includes both technical abilities – overall effectiveness of care – and personal treatment. As we will discuss in this chapter, retirement migrants from the Global North are positioned to benefit from wide access to high-quality healthcare services made more affordable to them than they might otherwise be by global divisions of wealth. This postcolonial relation to care persists even though most of these migrants do not recognise their privileges in this regard. They are more likely to attribute their access to high-quality care to cultural differences, that is, to a respect and love for older people that they believe is intrinsic to the cultures of their host nations. This cheaper and better treatment extends to the potential need for assistance in later life as well. Although health and assistance can be related, they do not need to be, and thus in this chapter, we distinguish between these two dimensions of precarity. Throughout, we also attend to the fact that underlying concerns for both healthcare and assistance is the reality that these migrants are older people; their age matters.

We begin this chapter, then, with a brief discussion of the ways in which age can influence health and healthcare, and is further shaped by the welfare state. Separately or in combination, health precarity can result. We will also argue that older age can impact the need for daily or intermittent support in later life, leading to what has been termed by Hall (2021) 'care precarity'. Throughout, we show how global inequalities present retirement migrants with ways to deal with these forms of precarity.

Age relations and the construction of health

Scholars have long recognised that health is socially constructed. Such social forces as relations of class, gender and age inequality combine with political economy, and professional organisations shape how we both understand and treat health and illness. These factors influence not only professional knowledge through 'assumptions about the prevalence, incidence, treatment, and meaning' of health and illness but also people's experiences of these (Brown, 1995: 34).

That age relations shape the social construction of health and thus health precarity has also been demonstrated repeatedly. A recent review of relevant literature makes clear that medical professionals behave differently with older patients, from diagnostics to communication to treatment (Wyman et al, 2018). The healthcare decisions made in the early weeks of the COVID-19 pandemic illustrated the long-time finding that medical professionals and others deem the lives of older people to be less valuable, and less worthy of medical expenditures, than those of younger people. Yet, it is not just in health crises that we see ageism but in daily medical decision-making as well.

For instance, research appearing in the *New England Journal of Medicine* showed that heart patients with birthdays on either side of 80 – two weeks before and two weeks after – received different medical treatment, with those two weeks shy of that birthday being far more likely to receive bypass surgery than those who had just turned 80 (Olenski et al, 2020). Age alone was sufficient to change medical judgements. Age may intersect with other statuses but remains an important social category in and of itself.

Health precarity in later life is also influenced by welfare states. Healthcare policies in both private and public spheres engage in ageism when they use age as a proxy for health conditions and as a basis for healthcare decisions and options (Calasanti and King, 2021). For instance, evidence from the UK suggests that a performance indictor sets death prior to age 75 to indicate 'premature death'. Here, the use of age, rather than health conditions, both treats the ageing of old people as a disease and indicates the lower value placed on those over age 75 (Wyman et al, 2018). In addition, Chapter 3 outlined the ways in which the health and care policies within the different nations examined here influence the risk of being (un)able to access healthcare and provide the backdrop for many retirement migrants' decisions to relocate. Taken together, older people face healthcare precarity not just in terms of potential access but also because ageism shapes experiences, including ultimate treatment, within these settings.

The impact of welfare state policies in shaping healthcare access for our retirement migrants is evident in cross-country comparisons. In Spain, Swiss and British retirees had either free or inexpensive access to the public healthcare system due to international agreements. Many of our interviewees found that the quality of care in the public system was good, and any delay in seeing a doctor could be shortened if one had private insurance, the cost of which they found to be inexpensive. For instance, Don explained that in addition to the public healthcare coverage he and his wife received thanks to the bilateral agreement between Spain and Switzerland, they opted to pay 200 euros per month for private healthcare for both of them. As a result, when he needed surgery, he was able to obtain it quickly in a private hospital because, he noted, in the public sector, "the delays are still rather long". Of course, retirement migrants' ability to afford private insurance was related to the relative economic power that they had gained by coming from a wealthy, colonising nation and then moving to Spain. Thus, their ability to afford private policies was much greater than for the majority of the local population.

By contrast, retirement migrants from the US, especially those 'health care refugees' (Miles, 2015: 43) who had been displaced from the labour market or had to retire early, did not have automatic access to healthcare, either in the US or abroad. The lack of universal health insurance in the US means that many people have to forgo or delay treatment prior to retirement age, and retirees are not covered by Medicare outside the US. This absence of healthcare coverage, in combination with high medical costs, placed US interviewees in a different position than the other interviewees, particularly the British, who had access to free healthcare.

For instance, Helen, a single, low-income retiree, had been coming to Mexico for dental and vision care for several years prior to her eventual migration. She described her previous experiences with dentistry in the US as a "calamity", as practitioner after practitioner subjected her to very expensive treatments that only made her problems worse. By contrast, she found that treatment in Mexico was both higher in quality and cheaper; she could afford to pay out of pocket to go through the process of fixing her teeth. She then asked her Mexican dentist to recommend an eye doctor, who subsequently took care of her cataracts. As a result of these positive interactions, she planned to establish her residency and then look into healthcare in Mexico. At the same time, she said that she was told by other migrants that, "If you have a thousand dollars in the bank, you're all set because [medical care is] very reasonable, anything you might need." As a result, she said that when she achieves her residency, she might stop paying into Medicare; since she could only access it in the US, she felt that she would not need it. At the same time, she was concerned about the costs of medical equipment, such as wheelchairs, that she might need, and she was worried about long-term care. The latter would be paid in the US by Medicaid for someone with her low income, whereas she was not sure how she would pay for it in Mexico.

Helen's story illustrates a couple of key points. First, even though she was not entitled to healthcare treatment in Mexico, she was still able to obtain good-quality care. Second, the notion that one did not need to be insured to receive good treatment was prevalent among the US migrants. Third, her discussion of the pros and cons of acquiring Mexican residency and health insurance, as well as continuing to pay into Medicare, made clear the considerations that retired migrants undertake for both healthcare and assistance in later life, and how they negotiate across welfare state policies.

In Costa Rica, US retirement migrants' access to healthcare was different still due to a combination of the policies of the host country and the infrastructure. As a result, our interviewees' experiences of healthcare in Costa Rica did not match the number one ranking accorded that country by International Living. They could access the public healthcare system, but the three towns where we conducted the interviews were remote, and the infrastructure for healthcare was very limited. For minor healthcare issues, pharmacies, as well as some medical clinics, provided access to inexpensive or free healthcare when they were covered by public insurance. More major issues were a different story. For instance, when Justin broke his leg, someone had to drive him four hours to the hospital in the capital city. Difficulty of travel and lack of nearby medical professionals or specialisations was also a concern. As Diane noted: "In Costa Rica, you have a heart attack, you call an ambulance, there're not coming. And if they come, it might just be a driver. ... There's nobody in the back." Thus, when faced with major healthcare issues, those over 65 years old and covered by Medicare flew back to the US for treatment. Some younger retirees paid for a private healthcare plan, while others just hoped that they would not need major treatments. Therefore, while accessing healthcare at low or no cost in Costa Rica was described by our interviewees as a big advantage as compared to the US, the limited access to medical care kept their health precarious.

Given that the availability and affordability of healthcare is a key concern to retirement migrants, potential host countries have touted the salubrious dimensions of migration to them (Miles, 2015). In addition to being of lower cost, healthcare is often hyped for being performed by practitioners who display more kindness, attention and concern than do their counterparts in the Global North. Such claims are embedded in promotional materials; Croucher (2022: 174) furnishes one example from a website, where readers are told: 'Medical care in Mexico today may remind you of an earlier period in your own life when a doctor took the time to actually sit down and listen to you.' Indeed, research shows that retirement migrants to the Global South feel that local professionals are friendlier and make more time for their older patients than doctors do in their home countries (see, for example, Benson, 2015; Miles, 2015; Hayes, 2018a). Some of our interviewees echoed this view, noting that they felt that they received healthcare that not only was highly effective but also attended to them as individuals. For instance, Don, a Swiss retirement migrant in Spain, said:

'It's not the public but the private healthcare system, [the medical practitioners] take the time. They take much more time [than in Switzerland]. They take the time to go and find the problems. ... And the dentist, it's the same thing. We also went through the dentist. So, the whole medical thing, it makes me feel very comfortable. I think it's one of the factors, one of the reasons why I don't plan to come back to Switzerland.'

Don contrasted the care he received in Spain as not only better but also not rushed; he felt that the medical staff were really taking the time they needed to address his concerns.

That said, retirement migrants are generally unaware that their economic and ethnic privileges relative to the local population shape these interactions and facilitate their care in their host countries. For example, Miles (2015) found that retirement migrants in Ecuador extoled the virtues of doctors there, noting that they spent a lot of time with their patients, made house calls and even gave out their phone numbers. She contrasts their timely and attentive care with that received by the local population: 'The average

Ecuadorian does not have the cell phone number of her doctor; and she waits in long lines to have 20 minutes of a doctor's time … if she is lucky' (Miles, 2015: 50). What the retirement migrants attribute to cultural differences in medical care reflects instead global relations that give them more disposable income than people in their host nations tend to have. Looking back at what Don said, we can see the difference that global inequalities made to the care he received. He made clear that he was speaking not of the public healthcare system but of that which he could access through paying for private insurance. Although the private system may seem inexpensive to him, this is because he had so much more economically than most of the local population. What he saved in living there rather than Switzerland could be used to pay for better care than might be obtained from the public system. Thus, Miles (2015) posits that the presence of more well-to-do retirement migrants might further erode the healthcare received by the local, poorer population, as medical practitioners seek more lucrative clients. In this way, retirement migrants can outbid local people and further degrade the care offered to the latter. In Mexico, globalisation in relation to healthcare is apparent not only in the medical tourism industry but also in US corporations building hospitals there 'to provide the best of both world[s]: "US-quality health care and low Mexican prices"' (Croucher, 2022: 173). As with Ecuador, catering to retirement migrants is likely to have a deleterious effect on local people's abilities to avail themselves of healthcare.

Loving care

Social and economic factors, as well as political contexts, also shape interpretations of abilities and the need for assistance and the ability to procure this (Hall, 2021). To be sure, the intensity of needs for support is high for infants and for some older people; however, the construction of such dependence and provision of assistance varies by age. As Fine (2021: 169, 176) aptly notes: 'Whether care is provided, and if so and by whom, are essentially social questions', and 'ideals and expectations held about care closely reflect the social context from which they arise'. The welfare state policies in the home countries we examined, including their assumptions about age, individual and family responsibilities, and gender, dictate both the extent to which assistance is valued and therefore given, and that families – typically female members – will provide it. The precarity of older people who need assistance emerges from the combined effects of the devaluation of old people and those who work to support them, and the lack of state funding for these services.

Grenier's (2021) analysis of frailty illustrates Fine's point in relation to older people's experiences of reduced abilities and precarity. They are aware that their vulnerabilities and losses, including the deaths of those around them, shape their needs. They also understand how their needs – which go beyond medical discourses and include help with shopping, meal preparation and the like, as well as social interaction – may be disconnected from their social resources and possibilities for support. Grenier's discussion makes clear that older people experience this situation in a larger context of ageism at the level of both welfare state policies and the handling of individual cases. The presentation of older people as a burden influences whether and how they respond to this disconnect by minimising their needs so as not to make demands or by feeling frustration or betrayal from 'being let down by a social contract that promised to provide' for them (Grenier, 2021: 73).

An illustration of this situation comes from Hall (2021), who documented the bases for what she refers to as 'care precarity' faced by British retirement migrants in Spain. As we have seen, these retirement migrants can receive healthcare through the public system. However, daily or intermittent assistance is not provided by the state because it assumes that care receivers will rely upon their families. Aside from the reality that not all older people have families, those of retirement migrants do not reside in Spain. Those retirement migrants with sufficient funds might be able to acquire private care, but not all will be able to afford this or have the funds for the long term. To deal with this precarity, Hall (2021) found that retirement migrants might rely on their social networks – relationships with other retirement migrants – to help fill in gaps in assistance. In our study, we saw evidence of this in Mexico, as several interviewees spoke of a woman who had recently broken her ankle. Some members of the community banded together to provide her meals and other assistance while she recovered. Relying on such networks for long-term support, however, especially among a group of same-aged persons who will also need assistance, does not remove precarity.

Global relations and local women as 'natural' caregivers

This precarity is situated in a context of the broader globalisation of markets, the outsourcing of care work and the interactions of global inequalities and gender relations that converge to 'solve' this 'problem' of assistance in later life through the work of the cheap labour of women from the Global South. Glenn (2010) discusses the ways neoliberalism and globalisation have shaped care work. In globalisation, wealthy nations outsource much of their production and increase service sector jobs. This reduces the availability of well-paying jobs with benefits and provides a growing array of low-waged, no-benefit jobs instead. At the same time, social welfare spending is reduced and public services are increasingly privatised. Meanwhile, in the Global South, neoliberal policies instituted by international financial institutions have also led to the loss of minimal government safety nets and the loss of agricultural land for subsistence agriculture so that export crops can be raised. The subsequent need for new sources of employment, combined with the need for service work, including care work that supports children and older people, has led women to migrate to new locales in the Global North where they are wanted for such work (Sassen, 2000).

Indeed, research on the need for assistance and migration has typically examined the movement of women from the Global South to the North to care for the children or ageing parents of women in wealthier countries who are themselves employed (Glenn, 2010; Fine, 2021). However, the impacts of globalisation and neoliberalism also results in retirement migrants looking to local women in their new countries to provide this labour at low cost. Whether in a new country or their own, women in/from the Global South are recruited – or, as Glenn (2010) maintains, coerced by the larger structures – to engage in assistance for (low) pay. Notably, such women are desired not only because of their low cost; Glenn argues that they are also seen to be better caregivers both as women and as coming from the Global South. Women are assumed to be 'natural' caregivers, while their location in the Global South marks them as coming from more traditional cultures where, it is assumed, elders are more respected and loved. The devaluation of care work further cheapens their labour, especially when performed for older people, and global inequalities exacerbate this (Calasanti, 2006; Glenn, 2010). Performing such work out of 'love', rather than 'skill', justifies low compensation. At the same time, the lack of state support makes it impossible for most older people, including those in the Global North, to afford to pay more. The result is the simultaneous devaluation of those who give and receive care.

Women from the Global South who give such support are also more likely to work without complaint and show deference (Glenn, 2010). As with our discussion of retirement migrants' perceptions of the greater respect granted to older people in their host countries and their positive impressions of healthcare providers, global inequalities likely underlie the deference they experience. These global relations intersect with gender relations in the Global South to influence retirement migrants' solutions to the precarity they face in terms of support needs.

Precarity and assistance in later life

That the treatment of older people who need support is problematic is apparent in the marketing in some of the countries in the Global South that targets this population. For instance, Croucher (2022: 177) notes that the '*Seniors Living Mexico* website advertised over 100 different facilities located throughout Mexico ranging from nursing homes and continuing care communities to in-home health aides, rehabilitation services, and medical tourism.' Again, the message is about not just the existence of options but the kind of support that will be provided. One website notes that in addition to the growing number of assisted living situations in Mexico, 'Others have chosen to have a live-in caretaker assume full responsibility 24/7. Mexican culture reveres those that have reached "la tercer edad" (the third age), and caring for senior citizens is not looked upon as a burden' (ElderGuru, 2020). These claims form the backbone of the response to criticisms that the movement of older people from the US to Mexico represented the 'outsourcing' of older people; the alternative, according to defenders, is 'warehousing': 'the options for older Americans with financial concerns narrow to warehousing or outsourcing' (Croucher, 2022: 177).

The vast majority of our respondents needed no daily assistance at the time of interview. Given that people from the Global North develop few difficulties prior to age 80, this is no surprise. However, many anticipated increasing needs for both healthcare and assistance, and the precarious nature of their handle on both. Jenny, from the US, had migrated to Costa Rica. She was only 63 but was concerned about her future. She could imagine living in Costa Rica as long as her health was good enough but wondered who would help her if she needed support. She had nephews in the US, and although she hoped that they would help her, they did not get along very well and she worried about how things would evolve should she live with one of them. She also considered moving to a different country, one that offered more options to older people in need of care. She thought about Spain but believed that the costs of living there were too high for her. Not having a clear view of her options for the future worried her.

For some of our respondents, moving to their host country was a way to meet their potential need for assistance. Angela (aged 75) and her husband William (aged 66) provide an apt illustration. Both former professionals from the US, Angela and William had been living in Mexico full-time for 12 years. They were drawn to the natural beauty and sense of community with new friends they met in the area, including other US migrants and locals. Angela emphasised the advantages of living in Mexico, noting that they did not pay a mortgage and there was little stress: "It's very relaxing. It's very caring." While describing Mexico as full of natural beauty and as a "whole other world", Angela also noted their ability to travel to the US when they wanted, including to continue to see her previous doctors for most of her healthcare. They sought medical care in Mexico on occasion, and Angela noted that the cost of such care was low: "It's like USD 3 to see a doctor."

Both Angela and William planned to stay in their home in Mexico when the time came for assistance with daily living. They had purchased their house, in part, because it had space to accommodate a live-in caregiver: "When you first come in, there's a room downstairs to the left of the front door with a bathroom. I thought, 'Well, this would be a good room for a caregiver, and then we never have to move again and we never have to leave here.'"

Both Angela and William spoke of the care that William's mother received after a head injury, contrasting her experiences in the US with those after they brought her to Mexico. First, Angela recounts:

'She was in a facility in [city], and you know, it was ching, ching, ching every time they practically turned her over. There was a period where she didn't eat, and they took her food to her. She was just a mess. We brought her down here [to Mexico], and she rallied. She was in a small facility. There were six people living there. The care she got was loving care. It wasn't, you know, antiseptic care or the sanitised care that you get in the US. It was loving care. They did her nails. They did her hair. They liked to dress her. She was lovely, beautiful woman. She was just taken such good care of. That, I think, was the other reason why we thought, "We can never go back [to the US]." Why would we? I would never. It was terrible to see the way she was living. It was terrible for me to hear the way people live that are older, and that the money they pay to do it.'

William echoed the sentiment:

'[My mom's situation] was a nightmare. It was a nightmare for a lot of reasons. … Even if there are a good set of roles or regulations, it all seems, in the end, very arbitrary about how people get treated and what decisions are made because you're not connected to anybody. … It was a terrible experience. I brought her here to Mexico. Old people are revered in Mexico.'

Angela's and William's views of their future assistance needs and plans dovetailed with Mexico's promotion of itself not only as an economic windfall for retirement migrants 'but also as a care paradise where Mexicans themselves are portrayed as inimitably warm, caring, and gladly willing to spend quality time with their foreign clientele' (Croucher, 2022: 173).

Angela's and William's accounts illustrate Glenn's (2010) main points concerning global relations and the personal (ADL) and instrumental (IADL) care provided by local women. The first is the economic dimension: the cheap cost of such assistance. Like Angela and William, some retirement migrants had purchased a home with the thought that it could house a live-in caregiver. In Costa Rica, David noted: "Our apartment has a little *casino* [living room] that we could make it so [a local woman] can stay there, and we would pay them so much a month and they would take care of us." In Mexico, Laura and her husband were among those interviewees with low incomes. Laura describes their house as conducive to living with declining abilities because they did not have many stairs and her husband could install railings. She also noted "a place where someone could, you know, a guest house so that somebody could stay there". Such care was less expensive in Mexico, she maintained. The intersecting global and gender relations that underlie the work performed by local women were especially apparent in Anna's assertion that should she need assistance in Mexico:

> 'I would have a hundred little girls come here every day. ... Okay? I have, at hand – I know [some of] my friends – like the 89-year-old has ... two girls every day, 24/7. The other one has 24/7, and the other one has 24/7. They're in their homes and these were not super-rich women, you know? It's affordable. USD 60 a day. ... And food's affordable. So ... if I had to have home care ... I would stay here.'

Even those with the lowest incomes spoke of the possibility of hiring local women, even if they could not afford it in the long term. Helen was single and could only afford to rent a small *casita* in Mexico. Still, as someone who had worked in a related medical field, she had seen nursing homes in the US and was clear that she wanted no part of that. She maintained that should she need care, "I would try to do what I see some people do here in Mexico ... hire people to come in and take care of me." She felt that her children would help with the cost as best they could and added: "I have always told them and thought to myself that I'd rather be crawling around than go to a nursing home [in the US]."

Helen's quote brings us back to the second point: the contrast between what Angela called the "antiseptic" care in the US and the "loving" care in Mexico. The perception that the local women who provide personal and instrumental assistance were also loving was ubiquitous, and respondents related their experiences to demonstrate this. Some had one or both parents cared for in Mexico, either in a facility (William) or in their home (Meredith and others), and extoled the virtues of the compassionate care they received. Carrie shared a story that undergirded her belief:

> 'Several of the people I know down here have home healthcare up to 24/7, and the people that take care of them are so wonderful; they become like family. One of our neighbours' sisters came down to die because she had ALS [amyotrophic lateral sclerosis], and she knew she was going to die and she knew she didn't want to do extreme measures. ... When she died, they had a little service for her, just on the front porch where she lived. I didn't know her that well, but I went to support the family. Her care workers were there, and they were all sobbing. I mean, this was part of their family that they lost, and that

was a big deal. It just made me feel like, "Wow, these are the people I want to have taking care of me when I'm a blithering idiot and can't get around, you know, and make sure I don't do anything too stupid." I just love the people down here and how gracious and caring they are.'

Of course, these depictions dovetail with Mexico's promotion of itself not only as an economic windfall for retirement migrants, 'but also as a care paradise where Mexicans themselves are portrayed as inimitably warm, caring, and gladly willing to spend quality time with their foreign clientele' (Croucher, 2022: 173). Jose, like many others, maintained that the care that older people receive in Mexico is both better quality and cheaper than in the US.

As we saw in Chapter 6, interviewees may have a glimmer of the global relations that make their care cheap; they accepted this as just the way things are and even see themselves as helping the local population. For example, when William talked about his future and their plans to hire someone to assist them, he said:

'I think it would actually be really nice to have a live-in person here, just to make it an advantage, not only for us but also for the person. If we could find someone where it would be truly beneficial because, as we get older, this is a big house.'

The notion of employing underpaid local women to provide care and assistance was part of the general belief that retirement migrants' presence was a positive force for the local people and economy by providing jobs and, in this instance, lodging. The gendered overlay of women as loving and natural caregivers, whose work is not really skilled, reinforces this belief and justifies their low pay. Gender inequalities found within all of the nations, both home and host, designate women for reproductive and domestic labour that pays less because women are supposed to do it naturally and largely out of love. The combined effect of these relations is to provide satisfying personal service at very low cost to the retirement migrants.

Finally, some interviewees could not foresee how they would address future healthcare needs, particularly if those became more regular or complex. This was particularly the case among low-income retirement migrants in Costa Rica. They found that given the lack of infrastructure, living in a remote, small town in Costa Rica was not compatible with such needs. At the same time, some could not really afford to move elsewhere. For instance, Jenny said that she could imagine living in Costa Rica as long as her health was good enough, but she wondered who would help her if she needed long-term care and support. Her hope that her nephews in the US would help was challenged by her realisation that she did not get along with them very well. She thought about moving to Spain but believed that the costs of living there were too high for her. Not having a clear view of her options for the future worried her. Several interviewees stated that they just hoped to stay healthy and die all of a sudden; others, as Miles (2015: 41) observed in Ecuador, simply 'refused to think that far into the future'.

Conclusion

In the countries of the Global North, from which our interviewees migrated, older people face precarity related to health and assistance that is contingent upon their age. That is to say, people of all ages can have health issues or need support; however, ageism influences the perception and treatment of these, such that older people's experiences are both different and more negative than those of younger adults. In this regard, age relations have at least two impacts. First, ageism shapes views of their health and need for support. Healthcare personnel can treat their maladies as less consequential (for example, 'just due to age') or less aggressively than they would if serving younger patients. Older people can be left feeling like their health is not taken as seriously as that of younger people. Second, welfare states provide variable protections or safety nets for older people who need healthcare or assistance with daily life. For instance, Medicare, the US programme of healthcare for older people, leaves large gaps in coverage (for example, vision or hearing care) and sometimes requires co-payments that are especially difficult for those who are economically precarious. Even countries like the UK, with wider healthcare coverage, often use the chronological age of the patient to guide the kind and extent of care that they give. Additionally, none of the welfare states in these home countries supply much in the way of assistance, especially long term. The idea of a country where healthcare is relatively cheap, where others avoid disparaging their health concerns and where medical personnel give them time and respect made for a powerful lure to many of our interviewees. In this regard, they took their global privileges for granted. That 'just three dollars' for a doctor might be out of reach for the local population was not remarked upon. Even those who might be more aware of the global relations that helped them tended not to acknowledge the way in which their presence might affect the ability of local people to receive equal care: they did not consider that their relative wealth made them more attractive customers to healthcare providers and could influence how they were treated. Interviewees assumed that the same quality of care was equally available to all and ascribed this egalitarian system to cultures that are more caring and more respectful of older people.

Likewise, loving domestic help and healthcare is an important advantage for retirement migrants. They help them to receive support without feeling like burdens or a social problem. Older people find themselves expected by governments to deploy personal strategies and avoid weighing down younger generations with demands for collective support (see Chapters 2 and 3). Living abroad, they can use their global power to answer this demand.

Again, it is not just 'antiseptic' care – impersonal healthcare – that our retirement migrants desired but 'loving care'. Given the ageism reviewed earlier, their need for assistance presents a constant threat to their personhood; they are at risk of so-called 'warehousing' or loss of autonomy. The romanticised marketing and perception of the local populations in retirement migrants' new countries serve as a counter to this form of precarity, and this was audible in our respondents' speculations about their future needs for assistance. They saw no way to meet those needs in their home countries. They feared becoming 'burdens' for their families at home, or never finding anyone to help them. Many hoped to stay as healthy as possible into the future and die 'suddenly', without ever needing help with everyday tasks. Yet, when they considered the latter option, they usually said that they planned to stay in Spain, Costa Rica and Mexico. Many planned to secure any help they would need by hiring cheap and 'loving' local, female workers, often as live-in caregivers who would support them in daily tasks. Some already employed domestic workers and emphasised the deference that their staff showed them and how this made them feel welcomed in their host country. As with healthcare or other goods and services that they consumed, the global inequalities that facilitated these retirement migrants' quality of life were far from their minds. Even the most financially precarious retirement migrants tended to have more economic power than local people, especially women, because of their financial basis in the Global North. Perhaps because of their own struggles, they could not see other power differentials or the privileges that those gave to them. Regardless of their own economic position, retirement migrants attributed the benefits of global relations to cultural differences and saw themselves as boons to the local economy and people, a view widely promoted by marketing materials from these countries.

8

Retirement migration, precarity and age

Introduction

Commenting upon precarity in later life, Fine (2021: 175) remarked recently: 'Risk among those of advanced age is not a matter of choice. Nor can it be reduced, it is argued, to an outcome of lifestyle options of individuals. It is instead produced by the sociocultural, economic and political environment, requiring political actions to address issues concerning inequality.' This book has sought to understand better how international retirement migration interacts with precarity in later life, and in doing so, it ultimately dovetails with Fine's observation. We built our study based on two observations. The first is that retirement migration is a growing phenomenon, one that scholars have often attributed to: (1) the increased buying power and resultant consumption among older people in countries of the Global North; (2) the globalisation of communications; and (3) the global leisure, healthcare and housing markets targeting older citizens of richer countries. Based on this, scholars have tended to view retirement migration as differing from the migration of younger people, in that it does not result from the search for better work conditions. Instead, retirees benefit from their pensions; they therefore diverge from younger people because they can use their economic power to relocate abroad and improve their lifestyles, particularly by consuming leisure and adventure. To do so, they move to poorer countries, either in the Global South or in European countries with lower costs of living, where they exploit the human, economic and natural resources of the host countries. In so doing, they also reproduce postcolonial power relations and structures (see, for example, Benson, 2013, 2015; Hayes, 2018a, 2018b). Based on these observations, many scholars depict retirement migration as a practice mostly performed by privileged older people who use their power for leisure purposes.

Second, other researchers argue that precarity increasingly shapes older people's lives in Global North countries, despite existing welfare state policies aimed at providing social protection to them. Drawing on the works of such scholars as Lain et al (2019, 2021) and Grenier et al (2021), we emphasised that such precarity can be economic, social or linked to needs for healthcare or assistance with daily life, and that these result from major transformations in the welfare state, the labour market and the household within a broader global context. A small but increasing number of researchers depict retirement migration as a strategy for people faced with precarity in later life to address these risks (see, for example, Bender et al, 2018; Hall, 2021). These authors argue that precarity in these contexts can persist or even return, typically when retirement migrants' healthcare needs increase (Ahmed and Hall, 2016). However, this literature is relatively marginal to the broader field of retirement migration, and the ways retirement migration and precarity interact have remained unclear.

We thus sought to examine more closely the links between retirement migration and precarity in later life. To do so, we studied retirees from three countries of the Global North – the UK, Switzerland and the US – who relocated permanently to three countries well known for retirement migration – Spain, Costa Rica and Mexico. Our participants resided in their new countries year-round, and they self-identified as 'retirees' even though some were too young to qualify for pension benefits. Our analysis drew on semi-structured interviews, as well as observations made during our stays in situ. In this final chapter, we summarise our findings, describe the limitations of our research and propose new questions that emerge from our study and are not answered by it.

Age came to the fore in an unexpected way. We did not anticipate the roles that age relations played in different forms of precarity. In retrospect and on the basis of our prior theorising of age relations, this should have been obvious; however, examining age inequality was not the original purpose of our study.

Economics and migration

Dovetailing with other recent studies and such scholars as Lain and colleagues (2019, 2021), we showed that retirement migration can be an answer to the economic precarity of later life that results from diverse social dynamics, such as the neoliberalisation of the labour market and the welfare state, particularly in its retirement and health policies, and transformations in the composition of families and households. Economic precarity can be a consequence of work lives shaped by external calamities, such as the recession of 2007–08. Those in retirement or about to retire face the potential loss of financial security based on the market performance of funds and savings; as we have shown, some of our respondents had counted on investments that disappeared during the crisis. As a result, many older people were left with incomes insufficient to ensure financial security in retirement. This economic disruption served to displace older workers, who were then unable to find good jobs and who were not yet old enough to receive a retirement pension. They may have left the labour market after years of poorly paid, insecure jobs, or they may have been forced to retire even though they were still too young to receive a pension and no longer had access to unemployment benefits. Such situations can also result from health problems that prevent people from continuing in paid employment.

Finally, ageism in the labour market can cause employers to lay off older workers whom they perceive as less productive or too costly even if productive. Some end up retiring early, such as Joan and Carl, and have sufficient incomes. However, others withdraw from the labour market even though they are not yet entitled to a retirement pension. Since their age inhibits them from finding secure jobs, they are 'retired' from the labour market despite being unable to qualify for retirement plans. As these people no longer have incomes, they mostly live on savings; relocating abroad allows them to live on limited money until they reach retirement age. The precarious ends to their careers also result in low retirement incomes, as these are based on earnings; this, in turn, may force them to continue living abroad after reaching pension eligibility.

These findings reinforce the claim made by some authors that retirement migration can be economically driven and serves as a response to insufficient income in later life. On these grounds, we urge that scholars of migration rethink the distinction often made between retirement migrants, who presumably relocate for leisure and lifestyle pursuits, and younger people who relocate for economic reasons.

However, retirement migrants are important actors for economies, just as are younger workers from the Global South who move to richer countries to work for low wages. Certainly, one could argue that consumption is an economic activity, and as both consumers and employers, older migrants often represent significant parts of the economies of receiving countries. Local and international companies, as well as states, advertise the loving care and economic and administrative incentives (tax breaks and easily accessible visas) that retirement migrants can find in these countries. They market towards those more well off, urging them to set up residence and invest in properties geared towards foreign retirees (see, for example, Croucher, 2022; Sunanta and Jaisuekun, 2022). Still, the outcomes for host countries are complex. Retirement migrants can create problems for the local population's economic security, limit their access to land and negatively affect public healthcare systems (see, for example, Miles, 2015; Hayes, 2018a, 2018b; Sunanta and Jaisuekun, 2022). At the same time, in the global capitalist economy, host states clearly want these retirees, as they bring money and provide both customers and employment for locals (Croucher, 2022).

Both younger people and retirement migrants migrate for economic reasons that are not just about consumption and leisure. Certainly, their situations vary, in that they are situated at different stages of the life course. However, retirement migrants, just like younger people, are part of the global economy, and both can be pursuing economic goals, particularly those who are precarious. To be sure, Hayes (2018a: 4) found that some retirement migrants call themselves 'economic refugees', meaning that they felt that they needed to move to cheaper countries to benefit from their lower costs of living and thus to enjoy greater adventures or leisure pursuits. However, for many retirees, migration is an economic strategy for survival and not just a means for 'active ageing'. Like younger migrants moving north, having enough money to live on is also a primary motivation. Retirement migrants are not necessarily moving to engage in paid labour; instead, they often relocate when they lack sufficient resources, sometimes as a result of age-related labour market displacement. These observations give weight to our belief that the classic distinction in the literature between younger 'economic' migrants and older 'leisure-lifestyle/amenity-seeking' retirement migrants is misleading. Rather than seeing these groups as distinct, scholars should consider their connections and how their different life stages matter. As we have shown, being unable to find good jobs in later life has pushed some older people to sell their homes (if they owned any) and relocate abroad. How does doing so matter? What difference does it make to be at a point in one's life where one cannot strategise moving elsewhere to find work and yet one is economically precarious? For many of the migrants we interviewed, economic precarity clearly led them to move. Some continued to work for small incomes where and when they could. When they look for lower costs of living, retirement migrants are also searching for more security, much like younger migrant workers. Depending on the research question at hand, exploring how age matters in driving migration and subsequent experiences might yield important insights. In this book, we have shown that to understand the economics behind retirement migration and precarity, it is important to situate retirement migrants within – rather than outside of – the global economy.

Social exclusion based on age

The most obvious way in which we found that age matters was in the revelation of the importance of ageism for understanding how retirement migration can aid in dealing with social precarity. As an oppression that affects all people as they age, ageism can lead to uncertainty about social status and future social relations, and thus the extent to which one feels included in the social milieu, regardless of economic status. Interviewees were aware of the ways in which their perceived age could influence negative treatment in their home countries; thus, a widely cited reason for their enjoyment in their new country was that they were respected and received better treatment, and that they were not perceived to be economic burdens. In their new locations, when their age was acknowledged, retirement migrants saw their age as providing benefits, such as preferential treatment in queues or senior discounts.

Perhaps the most revealing examples of the depth of ageism were the ways in which our interviewees talked about older people. Although they spoke of how nice it was to be surrounded by others of the same life stage or cohort, some also wanted not to be with old people all the time, or to seek out younger people. In this sense, like amenity-seeking retirement migrants, such as those studied by Hayes (2018a) in Ecuador, some of our interviewees sought to age successfully by trying to enact an active lifestyle – one that represents being 'not old' (Calasanti, 2016). Rather than just resulting from personal tastes and preferences, we found that this reflected age relations and retirement migrants' shared desire to live in a country where they would be respected and receive better treatment than in their home states, where they would be seen not as economic burdens but instead as contributors. Escaping ageism can take the form of new adventures, demonstrating to oneself and others that one is not old, or living in a place where retirement migrants feel more welcome and perceive old age not to be a problem. In all cases, ageism is an underlying thread, even if not a conscious concern. We found that ageism, or the worry that one will be excluded or treated differently because of age, undergirded other anxieties related to risks retirement migrants sought to avoid.

Health and assistance in later life

Our study allowed us to examine what health precarity entails in later life, as well as how this can shape retirement migration. Some research has shown that accessing healthcare at lower costs can be an important motivation for older people to relocate; further, the opportunity to do so rests upon global power relations and the exploitation of cheap healthcare workers in nations with less power (see, for example, Miles, 2015; Sunanta and Jaisuekun, 2022). Along these lines, some authors have indicated that the development of health and long-term care markets in the Global South has drawn support from richer states in the Global North willing to 'outsource' the health and support needs of their older populations to poorer countries (Ciafone, 2017: 155; Croucher, 2022). At the same time, such scholars as Schweppe (2022b) and Hall (2021) emphasise the insecure access to healthcare that retirement migrants may face, both in their home and in their host countries, for such reasons as insufficient incomes, lack of (adequate) health insurance and facilities, inadequate knowledge about the healthcare system, and poor mastery of the local language.

Our data help clarify how precarity can interact with health and assistance needs in later life. We showed that the precarity in this regard results from factors not under personal control; yet, they have an impact on older people's ability to access the healthcare and assistance they need (Fine, 2021). Inadequate public policies for healthcare and assistance, insufficient economic resources to pay for healthcare out of pocket or for private insurance, and the lack of kin living nearby and able to assist diminish older people's abilities to obtain care and retain dignity.

At the same time, age matters for the receipt of healthcare. Previous research has found that the concerns of older patients receive different, often lesser, treatment than those of younger people. Physicians may take them and their concerns less seriously; even the treatments themselves are changed based on perceived or chronological age. As with social inclusion in the broader milieu, being seen as less valuable than those who are younger can mean that older people are effectively excluded from good healthcare. Our respondents expressed pleasure not only with the effectiveness and cost of healthcare in their host countries but also with the ways healthcare practitioners treated them. In contrast to what they experienced in their home countries, they felt providers listened to and respected them; their problems were not simply ascribed to older age. They felt that they were treated as people whose health was worth defending.

Our study also makes clear that in the Global North, ageism influences precarity in accessing both healthcare and assistance for ADLs in later life. When they arise, older people's healthcare and daily support needs are treated both socially and politically as costly and burdensome, in contrast to other age groups, for whom such care is perceived as normal. Knowing that finding quality healthcare and assistance may be difficult, some older people move to new countries to find such care from medical practitioners and domestic workers who do not treat older people's needs as a problem. Retirement migration serves as a strategy for older people to overcome these precarities resulting from the policies (or lack thereof) and ageist treatment in the Global North.

At the same time, and as several scholars have noted, the ability to retire to a country that promotes itself as offering cheaper, loving care, even among those with low incomes, is a by-product of global power relations. Global inequalities allowed the retirement migrants we interviewed to improve their economic and health security, as well as to think about how they might obtain person-oriented support should they need it.

How these global relations also influenced social inclusion, especially in relation to mitigating ageism, is not so clear. As we have shown, living among peers and contributing to the local economy and the overall community helped our interviewees feel accepted and 'normal' in their new countries. They did not feel the marginalisation that goes with older age in their home countries. At the same time, much like others have shown (see, for example, Benson, 2013, 2015; Hayes, 2018a, 2018b, 2021), we found that what makes retirement migrants feel more valuable is tied to how locals treat them, interactions shaped by global power relations. Even though our interviewees rarely examined their privileges in this regard, their greater economic capital matters; they attributed their more positive experiences in relation to workers and the larger community to cultural differences. Whatever role culture plays, it cannot be divorced from the reality that even those with the lowest incomes had more resources than most of the local population. Allusions to '*gringo* pricing' hinted at an awareness of outsider status but inspired no greater reflection in our interviews, with the exception of Maggie. The extent to which social exclusion based on age was alleviated by migration in retirement is thus an open question, and answers may vary with time or context, a topic to which we return in the following.

Precarity, welfare states and retirement migration

Our book has sought to examine precarity in retirement migration contexts. Given the importance of welfare state policies related to such issues as retirement and healthcare (Estes and Wallace, 2010), we wanted to understand the extent to which and how these policies shaped our retirement migrants' decisions to relocate and their lives in their new country. We investigated retirees coming from three countries – the US, the UK and Switzerland – and sought to identify how their respective welfare state policies shaped migration and retirement.

First, our results made clear that retirement and health policies in home countries affect both migrants' decisions and their lives in their new countries. Many interviewees were concerned about retirement pension benefit levels, which were too low to cover basic necessities, such as housing, food and heating, in the home country. The welfare state policies in these countries are built on the expectation that people will contribute into an occupational or a private pension plan – or both – as well as savings. However, many of our participants had not had the chance to accumulate sufficient incomes by these means. Even in Switzerland, where occupational pensions are compulsory for certain workers and pension amounts are guaranteed by a federal law, our interviewees had not been able to contribute in a fashion that would give them financial security in later life; thus, economic concerns drove their migration. The inability to save for their lives in retirement resulted from diverse factors outside of their control, such as employment in low-paid jobs during their working years, losing part of their savings in a divorce or losing their savings in the 2007–08 financial crisis.

Second, we were surprised by how many participants left the labour market early, before reaching retirement age. Often left out of discussions of migration, these older displaced workers were unable to draw upon social insurance to tide them over until they reached retirement age. As a result, they relocated abroad. Respondents fortunate enough to have built up equity in housing in their home countries could sell their residences and use that money to see them through until they qualified for pensions; others had to be more creative, relying either on partners or on part-time, intermittent paid work. Of course, given the nature of the endings to their work careers, pension levels would be low as well. Moving to a new, cheaper country thus provided a minimal solution to economic precarity.

Third, healthcare policy concerns were critical but differed somewhat across the three countries. Since British participants could access healthcare for free in both the UK and Spain, they rarely mentioned the issues of affording healthcare in their home country as a major worry for them. However, some mentioned the quality of the healthcare system to be important, as they found it to be better in Spain, where they felt that medical staff spent more time with patients and they were able to obtain an appointment and care more quickly than in the UK.

In contrast to British participants, healthcare accessibility was a major concern to Swiss and US interviewees. Swiss respondents found that the universal, compulsory healthcare insurance in Switzerland was very expensive, and paying these out of retirement income was difficult, as the amount of the premiums and co-payments does not decrease after retirement. In addition, Swiss insurance includes coverage gaps, such as for dental or vision care, and paying for these out of pocket was a problem. In Spain, these issues were solved. Swiss retirement migrants no longer participated in the Swiss healthcare programme, but they could pay a low fee to join the Spanish public healthcare plan, and a supplemental insurance policy was relatively inexpensive. Healthcare was a significant issue for US participants as well, though in a way that differed somewhat from the Swiss. Interviewees younger than 65 years old were not old enough to be eligible for Medicare; to be covered by private health insurance would be quite expensive. Like the Swiss, many of those who were old enough to be covered by Medicare found that co-payments and other out-of-pocket costs were too high for them to afford, especially given that Medicare does not cover dental, vision or hearing needs. On one level, moving to a new country did not help US participants, as they were unable to access their healthcare benefits outside of the US. At the same time, and much like our other respondents, they found that healthcare costs in Mexico and Costa Rica were quite low, as were those for national healthcare insurance. Relatively easy eligibility criteria enhanced their ability to partake of these plans. Even paying for care without insurance, including dental, vision and hearing care, was manageable for those with the lowest incomes. Thus, moving to Mexico was a real boon for some of our US participants who could not afford healthcare in their home country.

Fourth, many participants were concerned about the needs for assistance in their daily lives that they had or anticipated needing the future. The fact that such support is not covered – or only very partially – by the welfare states in the three home countries meant that those interviewees who considered this issue sought to address this contingency on their own. As with income in later life, individuals are expected to take care of these issues; in this instance, states assume that families will provide such help. Of course, this requires the presence of family, the ability of family members to provide help and the willingness of older people to accept such aid. Again, older people have little control over diminished abilities that might result from advancing age. However, the fact that they were unable to secure access to such assistance in their home country meant that they would need to find a way to afford such support out of pocket, which they could do by relocating abroad.

As these observations show, welfare state policies have a strong influence on retirement migration, either because of how they work (for example, being strongly linked to labour pathways or asking insured people to pay for premiums and co-payment) or because they do not exist and leave people to deal with risks on their own. With the help of the marketing of receiving countries, who often have policies geared towards retirees from richer countries, retirement migrants can find ways to reduce these risks by relocating to countries where they can still receive their retirement pensions, where welfare states cover healthcare for free or at low cost, and where they can afford healthcare and assistance at low cost.

The dynamic nature of precarity

Finally, we found that the forms of precarity are dynamic. That is to say, retirement migration is often a temporary solution for precarity: it does not ensure that retirees will face no more economic or social risks, and the sense of security that it provides can disappear. New risks can surface as economic, political and social contexts fluctuate, or as people experience changes in their personal lives, such as in relation to family or health. Many, if not all, of these factors are outside of personal control. As a strategy to fight precarity, for most of our respondents, retirement migration will not work in the long run. We have described several examples of this unpredictability. The most obvious illustration is the Brexit vote in 2016, the impact of which was felt over time (Benson et al, 2022) and in our British respondents' lives. It led to heightened anxiety and feelings of insecurity, as they faced challenges to their economic status and new impediments to healthcare. Other socio-political issues were raised not only in light of Brexit but from seeing the direction governments were headed. For example, James, a US interviewee living in Mexico, was in good economic shape relative to many of his compatriots. However, he was also aware of how easily things could change:

> 'I live with this constant concern, it's a very quiet rumbling in the background, like concern that something isn't going right, type of thing. And it revolves around two issues. One is the government and

Mexico's relationship with the United States. And is something going to happen between those two governments that is going to screw up our lives here? Could they yank the bank trust, since we don't really own the property, this is kind of loaned to us, in a sense, through a bank trust. So, unless I become a citizen of Mexico, I can't really own this. So, there's that constant undercurrent of, you know, what happens if we get to be in, now we're maybe in, our late 80s or something like that and that happens … what the hell do we do?'

Retirement migration does not protect from social precarity in the long term, and our respondents might find that the respect they received from locals might disappear if their economic situation or the social context in their new country worsened. For instance, after living in Costa Rica for a couple of years, Diana learned that the sense of inclusion that she felt as a result of living mostly among retirement migrants changed when younger 'digital nomads' relocated to her town in large numbers. Before, she felt that she was living mostly with "all white-haired people … old people", a generation of which she felt a part. When younger people started settling there, Diana felt much less accepted and experienced age-based verbal abuse. In our second interview, she spoke of how retirement migrants complained about younger migrants organising loud and crowded parties near their neighbourhoods at night. She reported that the younger people's reactions clearly reflected ageism. She described the interactions that had occurred in this context wherein younger migrants told their older counterparts, ' "Oh, you're old, be quiet", that kind of stuff. … It was very rude. "Move out of town, move away, do something." You know, I was told to move away, and I was like, "I don't live in town, I live [in the next village], and I still hear you." '

Just like economic and social precarity, uncertainties regarding future healthcare and assistance persist among retirement migrants, as other scholars have highlighted (see, for example, Miles, 2015; Hall, 2021; Schweppe, 2022a). In this book, we have shown that many retirement migrants are unsure what they would do if they needed extended healthcare in the future, especially long-term care. Women are especially concerned about this issue, as they are more likely to provide care in later life and to be faced with their own care needs without having a partner to rely on. Although they sometimes consider this as they search for new residences, they often do not know how they will deal with such needs in the future. Some hope to remain in good physical shape until death, and some imagine returning to their home countries if they need extended care. At the same time, those who cannot afford such care at home, including those who have nobody to rely on for support, are often concerned about their health in the future. Some just do not want to think about it. Again, retiring abroad can secure their access to healthcare and assistance with daily life, but how much and how long this will continue are unclear. Retirement migration has provided a respite from precarity that is temporary at most.

Implications for the future

We do not claim that our data are representative. Regardless of that, our findings have important implications. First, we should not presume that all retirement migrants are comfortable seekers of greater amenities. No doubt, some who are not economically precarious are trying to enact a particular, more privileged lifestyle and often for lower costs. We certainly saw evidence of this in our study. However, these so-called 'lifestyle migrants' were in the minority in our sample. Instead, the majority of our respondents were anxious over their economic precarity. Although other researchers have pointed to the economic precarity of some retirement migrants, their prevalence in our sample was remarkable and likely reflects the broader global economic and welfare state austerity that increases their numbers. Heretofore, this group have received little scholarly attention, perhaps because they fall into a nowhere land of being too old to be employed in decent jobs and too young to qualify for retirement benefits. They were simply out of the labour force. We found that both of these anxious groups – those waiting for benefits and those collecting – wound up economically precarious due to circumstances beyond their control: economic recession, downsizing and labour market discrimination. We did not seek out this group for our research; it is possible that our focus on those who had moved permanently excluded wealthier people who have retained residences in their home countries. Nevertheless, the fact that we found so many economically precarious retired migrants seems noteworthy. As foreshadowed by the work of such scholars as Lain and colleagues (2019, 2021), Macnicol (2015), Polivka and Luo (2021) and Phillipson (2021), they are caught in the vicissitudes of globalisation and changing economies, welfare state contraction, and changing households.

Age relations and the ageism that they generate play a vital, if often covert, role in the experiences of retirement migrants. Not only did ageism push many of our respondents out of the labour market, where some had more cushion than others, but being older can result in social exclusion, less access to or lower-quality healthcare, and limited assistance in later life. Dealing with these forms of precarity became easier for some of our interviewees when they moved to new countries, where they found age peers and greater respect for older people, more accessible and attentive healthcare providers, and possibilities for support in living their final years with dignity.

Retirement migration cannot be understood without looking at how countries of the Global North treat old age. This shifts our research gaze away from seeing retirement migration as reflecting personal tastes in leisure consumption (moving closer to nature, discovering other cultures or embarking on new adventures) and looking at more structural factors. Thus, examining retirement migration trends includes considering welfare state policies in both home and receiving countries, as well as how age relations and other inequalities shape older people's experiences. This includes the understanding that in many countries of the Global North, welfare states are contracting, limiting their role in providing basic supports and placing the onus for security on older people and their families. Older people understand this well, and retiring abroad is one option they consider in meeting this demand.

Given the dynamic nature of precarity, however, this solution is temporary. The occurrence of Brexit while we conducted our interviews made this clear; economic, structural and global changes are outside of personal control. Even health changes can increase precarity – not so much because of the direct effects of injury and disease but due to the impact of ageism and the lack of support that make these changes all the more frightening. As the opening quote for this chapter asserts, older people's precarity does not result from the personal decisions or intentions of those most at risk of loss.

This brings us to our final observation. As other scholars have noted, the ability of retirement migrants to push against these forms of precarity comes at the expense of local people and economies who are themselves made precarious by the presence of retirement migrants. However, this situation is not as straightforward as it might appear. Retirement migration is at the nexus of local and global power relations, with far-reaching implications and ramifications. Marginalised people in both the Global North and South are dealing with structural inequality and pay the price of globalisation. Both are dealing with situations that are outside of their immediate control. To be sure, global power relations provide even the most economically precarious retirement migrants with 'relative privilege' (Benson, 2015: 21) and allow them to search for better lives in cheaper countries. At the same time, retirement migrants – themselves marginalised by age and other inequalities – who seek to help local people by volunteering for local organisations and groups, by providing jobs, and so on do not change the global relations in which they are embedded.

In terms of social justice, then, our findings point to the inadequacy of an age-inflected global system, in which economically advantaged countries in the Global North can outsource their older citizens to poorer countries, rather than providing them with the means for decent lives at home. As Croucher (2022) noted, governments in the Global North are quite aware of the advantages of having their citizens retire abroad. At the same time, governments in poorer nations seek to attract these retirees. They market healthcare and assistance, as well as lifestyle, to older people migrating from the Global North, just as locals in these same countries are pushed to migrate North to care for older people there in order to survive economically. This system relies on the exploitation of less powerful countries, along with the exclusion of less privileged older people in richer states, who are told that they must take responsibility for their needs as they age by relocating abroad. Otherwise, they must face precarious economic and social conditions in their home countries. Intersecting power relations based on systems of both global and age inequalities are therefore central to understanding retirement migrants' experiences and motivations, both in their home states and in their host countries.

Notes

Chapter 1
1. In this book, we use the terms 'retirement migration' and 'international retirement migration' interchangeably, as our book focuses only on this type of movement.
2. Our calculation is based on data from the UN (2019).
3. We use 'home' and 'host' countries to depict the country in which retirement migrants lived prior to migration and the country in which they have relocated in retirement, respectively.

Chapter 3
1. Government-produced data reflect certain modes of calculation, which can vary between countries. Therefore, in this chapter, we use OECD data to compare between countries. These data can differ slightly from data produced by national governments.
2. However, this depends on how the 'official' poverty rate is measured, which is an issue in these countries.
3. Available at: www.legislation.gov.uk/ukpga/2008/14/section/9/enacted (accessed 23 July 2022).
4. In Switzerland, the Confederation is the national-level institution. It is composed of cantons, which are local states provided with a certain level of political autonomy.
5. In 2020, the state financed 20 per cent of the insurance (Loi sur l'Assurance-vieillesse et survivants [LAVS], Article 103).
6. In 2020, this amount was 21,330 Swiss francs (equivalent to around £19,170). See 'Loi fédérale sur la prévoyance professionnelle vieillesse, survivants et invalidité'. Available at: www.admin.ch/opc/fr/classified-compilation/19820152/index.html#fn-#a (accessed 15 July 2020).
7. Just under one quarter of retirees do receive supplemental health insurance coverage from their previous employers or unions (Federal Interagency Forum on Aging Related-Statistics, 2020: 122).
8. People over 65 not entitled to SS can pay premiums to obtain Medicare coverage.
9. There is also a coverage gap, wherein Part D participants must pay the total cost of their drugs once they surpass a certain limit each year, until they reach a level wherein coverage resumes (Medicare.gov, no date).

Chapter 6
1. Although she was eligible to receive SS, she had not reached age 66, the age at which she would receive a full benefit. Many people in the US seem unaware that the full benefit age rose from 65, a number still commonly used to depict old age.

References

Acker, L. and Dwyer, P. (2004) 'Fixed laws, fluid lives: the citizenship status of post-retirement migrants in the European Union', *Ageing and Society*, 24(3): 451–75.

Ahmed, A. (2015) *Retiring to Spain: Women's Narratives of Nostalgia, Belonging and Community*, Bristol: Policy Press.

Ahmed, A. and Hall, K. (2016) 'Negotiating the challenges of ageing as a British migrant in Spain', *GeroPsych: The Journal of Gerontopsychology and Geriatric Psychiatry*, 29(2): 105–14.

Alexander, J. and Fernandez, K. (2021) 'The impact of neoliberalism on civil society and nonprofit advocacy', *Nonprofit Policy Forum*, 12(2): 367–94.

Anchisi, A. and Despland, B. (2010) 'Les proches d'un parent âgé dépendant: le cœur du dispositif de l'aide et des soins à domicile en Suisse', in A. Blanc (ed) *Les Aidants Familiaux*, Grenoble: Presses Universitaires de Grenoble, pp 177–97.

Balmer, I. and Gerber, J.D. (2018) 'Why are housing cooperatives successful? Insights from Swiss affordable housing policy', *Housing Studies*, 33(3): 361–85.

Bantman-Masum, E. (2015) 'Les Étatsuniens de Mérida, Mexique: mobilité ou migration?', *Revue Européenne des Migrations Internationales*, 31(2): 119–38.

Barbosa, B., Amaral Santos, C. and Santos, M. (2021) 'Tourists with migrants' eyes: the mediating role of tourism in international retirement migration', *Journal of Tourism and Cultural Change*, 19(4): 530–44.

Béland, D. (2002) 'Les paradoxes de la privatisation: Épargne individuelle et réforme des retraites aux États-Unis', *Revue française des affaires sociales*, 1: 91–108.

Bell, C. (2017) 'We feel like the King and Queen', *Asian Journal of Social Sciences*, 45(3): 271–93.

Bender, D. and Schweppe, C. (2022) '"Between heaven and hell": love, sex and intimacy: international retirement migration of older men to Thailand', in C. Schweppe (ed) *Retirement Migration to the Global South: Global Inequalities and Entanglements*, Singapore: Palgrave Macmillan, pp 117–38.

Bender, D., Hollstein, T. and Schweppe, C. (2017) 'The emergence of care facilities in Thailand for older German-speaking people: structural backgrounds and facility operators as transnational actors', *European Journal of Ageing*, 14: 365–74.

Bender, D., Hollstein, T. and Schweppe, C. (2018) 'International retirement migration revisited: from amenity seeking to precarity migration?', *Transnational Social Review*, 8(1): 98–102.

Benson, M. (2011) 'The movement beyond (lifestyle) migration: mobile practices and the constitution of a better way of life', *Mobilities*, 6(2): 221–35.

Benson, M. (2013) 'Postcoloniality and privilege in new lifestyle flows: the case of North Americans in Panama', *Mobilities*, 8(3): 313–30.

Benson, M. (2015) 'Class, race, privilege: structuring the lifestyle migrant experience in Boquete, Panama', *Journal of Latin American Geography*, 14(1): 19–37.

Benson, M. and O'Reilly, K. (2009) 'Migration and the search for a better way of life: a critical exploration of lifestyle migration', *The Sociological Review*, 57(4): 608–25.

Benson, M., Zambelli, E., Carven, C. and Sigona, N. (2022) 'British citizens in the EU after Brexit', *Migzen Research Brief*, 1. Available at: https://policycommons.net/artifacts/2389486/benson_et_al__2022_british_citizens_in_the_eu_after_brexit/3410671/ (accessed 18 December 2022).

Bolzman, C. (2021) 'Linked lives, dividing borders: from transnational solidarity to family reunification of an older parent', in M. Repetti, T. Calasanti and C. Phillipson (eds) *Ageing and Migration in a Global Context: Challenges for Welfare States*, Cham: Springer, pp 97–111.

Bolzman, C., Fokkema, T. and van Dalen, D. (2022) 'Transnational social relationships of international retirement migrants in Morocco: a typology', in C. Schweppe (ed) *Retirement Migration to the Global South: Global Inequalities and Entanglements*, Singapore: Palgrave Macmillan, pp 139–61.

Botterill, K. (2017) 'Discordant lifestyle mobilities in East Asia: privilege and precarity of British retirement in Thailand', *Population, Space and Place*, 23(5): 1–11.

Bozio, A., Crawford, R. and Tetlow, G. (2010) *The History of State Pensions in the UK: 1948 to 2010*, Swindon: Economic and Social Research Council.

Brook, J. and Jackson, D. (2020) 'Older people and COVID-19: isolation, risk and ageism', *Journal of Clinical Nursing*, 29(13–14): 2044–6.

Brown, P. (1995) 'Naming and framing: the social construction of diagnosis and illness', *Journal of Health and Social Behavior*, extra issue: 34–52. Available at: https://doi.org/10.2307/2626956 (accessed 17 August 2022).

Bureau of Labor Statistics (2017) Employment projections, civilian labor force participation rate by age, sex, race, and ethnicity. Availble at: www.bls.gov/emp/tables/civilian-labor-force-participation-rate.htm (accessed 21 February 2023).

Butler, R.N. (1975) *Why Survive? Being Old in America*, New York: Harper and Row.

Bytheway, B. (1995) *Ageism*, Buckingham: Open University Press.

Calasanti, T. (2005) 'Ageism, gravity, and gender: experiences of aging bodies', *Generations*, 29(3): 8–12.

Calasanti, T. (2006) 'Gender and old age: lessons from spousal care work', in T. Calasanti and K.T. Slevin (eds) *Age Matters: Realigning Feminist Thinking*, New York, NY, and London: Routledge, pp 269–94.

Calasanti, T. (2016) 'Combating ageism: how successful is successful aging?', *The Gerontologist*, 56(6): 1093–101.

Calasanti, T. (2020) 'Brown slime, the silver tsunami, and apocalyptic demography: the importance of ageism and age relations', *Social Currents*, 7(3): 195–211.

Calasanti, T. and King, N. (2017) 'Successful aging, ageism, and the maintenance of age and gender relations', in S. Lamb (ed) *Successful Aging as a Contemporary Obsession: Global Perspectives*, New Brunswick, NJ: Rutgers University Press, pp 27–40.

Calasanti, T. and King, N. (2021) 'Beyond successful aging 2.0: inequalities, ageism, and the case for normalizing old age', *The Journals of Gerontology. Series B, Psychological Sciences and Social Sciences*, 76(9): 1817–27.

Calasanti, T. and Repetti, M. (2018) 'Swiss retirees as active agers: a critical look at this new social role', *Journal of Population Ageing*, 11(1): 23–41.

Calasanti, T. and Slevin, K. (2006) *Age Matters: Re-Aligning Feminist Thinking*, New York: Routledge.

Calzada, I. and Gavanas, A. (2018) 'The market value of trans-cultural capital: a case study of the market of provision for Scandinavian retirement migrants in Spain', *Journal of Ethnic Migration Studies*, 46(19): 4142–59.

Castles, S., de Haas, H. and Miller, M.J. (2014) *The Age of Migration*, Houndmills: Palgrave Macmillan.

Ciafone, A. (2017) 'The third age in the Third World: outsourcing and outrunning old age to The Best Exotic Marigold Hotel', in S. Chivers and U. Kriebernegg (eds) *Care Home Stories*, Bielefeld: Transcript Verlag, pp 155–74.

Cohen, S.A., Duncan, T. and Thulemark, M. (2015) 'Lifestyle mobilities: the crossroads of travel, leisure and migration', *Mobilities*, 10(1): 155–72.

Convention de sécurité sociale entre la Confédération suisse et l'Espagne (1969) 'Convention de sécurité sociale entre la Confédération suisse et l'Espagne'. Available at: https://suizosdevalencia.org/wp-content/uploads/2018/11/Seguro-Social-Sozialversicherungsbkommen_CH_ES_FR.pdf (accessed 23 July 2022).

Cornwell, B., Laumann, E.O. and Schumm, L.P. (2008) 'The social connectedness of older adults: a national profile', *American Sociological Review*, 73(2): 185–203.

Croucher, S. (2022) 'International living (and dying). U.S. retirement migration in Mexico', in C. Schweppe (ed) *Retirement Migration to the Global South: Global Inequalities and Entanglements*, Singapore: Palgrave Macmillan, pp 165–85.

Crystal, S., Shea, D.S. and Reyes, A.M. (2016) 'Cumulative advantage, cumulative disadvantage, and evolving patterns of late-life inequality', *The Gerontologist*, 57(5): 910–20.

Dallera, C., Hugentobler, V. and Anchisi, A. (2014) 'L'apparition d'organisations marchandes dans le domaine de l'aide et des soins à domicile en Suisse romande: Nouveaux enjeux pour lesterritoires ou redéfinition des territoires de l'aide et des soins de longue durée?', *SociologieS*. Available at: http://journals.openedition.org/sociologies/4848 (accessed 23 July 2022).

Dallera, C., Palazzo-Crettol, C. and Anchisi, A. (2015) 'Accompagner des personnes âgées en couple: un angle mort du travail social', *Service Social*, 61(1): 1–18.

Dannefer, D. (2020) 'Systemic and reflexive: foundations of cumulative disadvantage and life-course processes', *The Journals of Gerontology: Series B*, 75(6): 1249–63.

Dannefer, D. and Huang, W. (2017) 'Precarity, inequality, and the problem of agency in the study of the life course', *Innovation in Aging*, 1(3): 1–10.

De São José, J.M.S. and Calasanti, T. (2023) 'Ageism as discriminatory practices: a response to the tripartite definition', unpublished manuscript.

Dickman, S., Himmelstein, D. and Woolhandler, S. (2017) 'America: equity and equality in health 1: inequality and the health-care system in the USA', *The Lancet*, 389: 1431–41.

ElderGuru (2020) Eldercare and assisted living in Mexico for expats. Available at: www.elderguru.com/eldercare-assisted-living-mexico/ (accessed 27 July 2022).

Estes, C.L. (2004) 'Social security privatization and older women: a feminist political economy perspective', *Journal of Aging Studies*, 18(1): 9–26.

Estes, C.L. and Phillipson, C. (2002) 'The globalization of capital, the welfare state, and old age policy', *International Journal of Health Services*, 32(2): 279–97.

Estes, C.L. and Wallace, S.P. (2010) 'Globalization, social policy, and ageing: a Northern American perspective', in D. Dannefer and C. Phillipson (eds) *The Sage Handbook of Social Gerontology*, London: Sage, pp 513–24.

Estes, C.L., Biggs, S. and Phillipson, C. (2003) *Social Theory, Social Policy and Ageing: A Critical Introduction*, Maidenhead: Open University Press.

Eur-Lex (2004) 'Regulation (EC) No. 883/2004 of the European Parliament and of the Council of 29 April 2004: Document 02004R0883-20190731'. Available at: https://eur-lex.europa.eu/legal-content/EN/TXT/PDF/?uri=CELEX:02004R0883-20190731&from=EN (accessed 23 July 2022).

Federal Interagency Forum on Aging-Related Statistics (2020) *Older Americans 2020: Key Indicators of Well-Being*, Washington, DC: US Government Printing Office.

Federal Social Insurance Office (2016) *La Prévoyance Professionnelle. Le Deuxième Pilier de la Prévoyance Vieillesse, Survivants et Invalidité Après la Première Révision de la LPP*, Bern: Federal Social Insurance Office. Available at: www.bsv.admin.ch/dam/bsv/fr/dokumente/bv/merkblaetter/die_berufliche_vorsorgenachder1bvgrevision.pdf.download.pdf/la_prevoyance_professionnelleapresla1rerevision.pdf (accessed 23 July 2022).

Federal Social Insurance Office (2023) *Stabilisation de l'AVS*, Bern: Federal Social Insurance Office. Available at: https://www.bsv.admin.ch/bsv/fr/home/assurances-sociales/ahv/reformes-et-revisions/ahv-21.html (accessed March 16 2023).

Fine, M. (2021) 'Reconstructing dependency: precarity, precariousness and care in old age', in A. Grenier, C. Phillipson and RA. Setterseten (eds) *Precarity and Aging: Understanding Insecurity and Risk in Later Life*, Bristol: Policy Press, pp 169–90.

Fraser, D. (2003) *The Evolution of the British Welfare State*, Champ: Springer.

Gambold, L. (2013) 'Retirement abroad as women's aging strategy', *Anthropology and Aging Quarterly*, 34(2): 184–98.

Gatrell, P. (2019) *The Unsettling of Europe. The Great Migration, 1945 to the Present*, London: Penguin.

Gavanas, A. (2017) 'Swedish retirement migrant communities in Spain: privatization, informalization and moral economy filling transnational care gaps', *Nordic Journal of Migration Research*, 7(3): 165–71.

Gehring, A. (2016) 'Dutch retirement migration to Spain and Turkey: seeking access to healthcare across borders', *Transnational Social Review*, 6(3), 326–43.

Gehring, A. (2017) 'Pensioners on the move: a "legal gate" perspective on retirement migration to Spain', *Population, Space and Place*, 23(5): 1–11.

Gibbons, H.M. (2016) 'Compulsory youthfulness: intersections of ableism and ageism in "successful aging" discourses', *Review of Disability Studies*, 12(2–3): 1–19.

Gilleard, C. and Higgs, P. (2005) *Contexts of Ageing*, Cambridge: Polity Press.

Glenn, E.N. (2010) *Forced to Care: Coercion and Caregiving in America*, Cambridge: Harvard University Press.

Gottfried, H. (2013) *Gender, Work, and Economy: Unpacking the Global Economy*, Cambridge: Polity.

Gov.UK (2017) Proposed new timetable for state pension age increases. Available at: www.gov.uk/government/news/proposed-new-timetable-for-state-pension-age-increases (accessed 23 July 2022).

Gov.UK (2019) Healthcare for UK nationals living in Spain. Available at: www.gov.uk/guidance/healthcare-in-spain-including-the-balearic-and-canary-islands (accessed 23 July 2022).

Gov.UK (2022) Pension Credit. Available at: www.gov.uk/pension-credit (accessed 23 July 2022).

Grenier, A. (2021) 'Rereading frailty through a lens of precarity: an explication of politics and the human condition of vulnerability', in A. Grenier, C. Phillipson and A. Richard (eds) *Setterseten in Precarity and Aging: Understanding Insecurity and Risk in Later Life*, Bristol: Policy Press, pp 69–90.

Grenier, A. and Phillipson, C. (2018) 'Precarious aging: insecurity and risk in late life', *Hasting Center Report*, 48(5: What Makes a Good Life in Late Life? Citizenship and Justice in Aging Societies): 15–18.

Grenier, A., Phillipson, C., Rudman, D.L., Hatzifilalithis, S., Kobayashi, K. and Marier, P. (2017) Precarity in late life: understanding new forms of risk and insecurity, *Journal of Aging Studies*, 43: 9–14.

Grenier, A., Hatzifilalithis, S., Laliberte-Rudman, D., Kobayashi, K., Marier, P. and Phillipson, C. (2020) Precarity and aging: a scoping review, *The Gerontologist*, 60(8): 620–32.

Grenier, A., Phillipson, C. and Settersten, R. (2021) 'Precarity and ageing: new perspectives for social gerontology', in A. Grenier, C. Phillipson and R. Settersten (eds) *Precarity and Ageing: Understanding Insecurity and Risk in Later Life*, Bristol: Policy Press, pp 1–17.

Guo, H.J. and Sapra, A. (2020) *Instrumental Activity of Daily Living*, Treasure Island, FL: StatPearls. Available at: www.ncbi.nlm.nih.gov/books/NBK553126 (accessed 23 July 2022).

Gustavson, P. (2008) 'Transnationalism in retirement migration: the case of North European retirees in Spain', *Ethnic and Racial Studies*, 31(3): 451–75.

Haber, C. and Gratton, B. (1993) *Old Age and the Search for Security: An American Social History*, Bloomington, IN: Indiana University Press.

Hall, K. (2021) 'Care precarity among older British migrants in Spain', *Ageing and Society*, 1–19. Available at: https://doi.org/10.1017/S0144686X21001392 (accessed 7 July 2022).

Hall, K. and Hardill, I. (2016) 'Retirement migration, the "other" story: caring for frail elderly British citizens in Spain', *Ageing and Society*, 36(3): 562–85.

Hardill, I., Spradbery, J., Arnold-Boakes, J. and Marrugat, M. (2005) 'Severe health and social care issues among British migrants who retire to Spain', *Ageing and Society*, 25(5): 769–83.

Hayes, M. (2015) 'Moving south: the economic motives and structural context of North America's emigrants in Cuenca, Ecuador', *Mobilities*, 10(2): 267–84.

Hayes, M. (2018a) *Gringolandia: Lifestyle Migration under Late Capitalism*, Minneapolis, MN: University of Minnesota Press.

Hayes, M. (2018b) 'The gringos of Cuenca: how retirement migrants perceive their impact on lower income communities', *Area*, 50(4): 467–75.

Hayes, M. (2021) '"Sometimes you gotta get out of your comfort zone": retirement migration and active ageing in Cuenca, Ecuador', *Ageing and Society*, 41(6): 1221–39.

History of Social Security in Switzerland (2020) Old age provision. Available at: www.historyofsocialsecurity.ch/risk-history/old-age-provision (accessed 23 July 2022).

Hochschild, A.R. (2014) 'Global care chains and emotional surplus value', in D. Engster and T. Metz (eds) *Justice, Politics, and the Family*, New York, NY: Routledge, pp 256–68.

Huber, A. (1999a) *Heimat in der Postmoderne*, Zurich: Seismo Verlag.

Huber, A. (1999b) *Ferne Heimat: Zweites Glück? Sechs Porträts von Schweizer Rentnerinnen und Rentnern an der Costa Blanca*, Zurich: Seismo Verlag.

Huber, A. (2003a) *Sog des Südens: Altersmigration von der Schweiz nach Spanien am Beispiel Costa Blanca*, Zurich: Seismo Verlag.

Huber, A. (2003b) *Auswandern im Alter. Acht Lebensgeschichten von Schweizer Senioren an der Costa Blanca: Ein Lese- und Informationsbuch*, Zurich: Seismo Verlag.

Huber, A. and O'Reilly, K. (2004) 'The construction of Heimat under conditions of individualised modernity: Swiss and British elderly migrants in Spain', *Ageing and Society*, 24(3): 327–51.

Hunter, A. (2018) 'Older migration: inequalities of ageing from a transnational perspective', in S. Westwood (ed) *Ageing, Diversity and Equality: Social Justice Perspectives*, London: Routledge, pp 195–209.

Hurd, L. (1999) '"We're not old!": older women's negotiations of aging and oldness', *Journal of Aging Studies*, 13(4): 419–39.

International Living (no date) One of the best places in the world to retire is Mexico. Available at: https://internationalliving.com/countries/mexico/retire/ (accessed 23 July 2022).

International Living (2020) Costa Rica has excellent health care. Available at: https://internationalliving.com/countries/costa-rica/health-care/ (accessed 23 July 2022).

International Living (2021) 6 countries with the best healthcare in the world. Available at: https://internationalliving.com/countries-best-healthcare-world/ (accessed 17 August 2022).

International Living (2022) We swapped the American Dream for a dream life in Costa Rica. Available at: https://internationalliving.com/we-swapped-the-american-dream-for-a-dream-life-in-costa-rica/ (accessed 23 July 2022).

IOM (International Organisation for Migration) (2020) 'Migration data portal'. Available at: www.migrationdataportal.org/international-data?i=stock_abs_&t=2020 (accessed 5 June 2020).

Kalleberg, A.L. (2018) *Precarious Lives: Job Insecurity and Well-Being in Rich Democracies*, Cambridge: Polity Press.

Kam, V.A. (1977) *Retiring to the Seaside*, London: Routledge and Kegan Paul.

Katz, S. (2000) 'Busy bodies: activity, aging, and the management of everyday life', *Journal of Aging Studies*, 14(2): 135–52.

Katz, S. and Calasanti, T. (2015) 'Critical perspectives on successful aging: does it "appeal more than it illuminates"?', *The Gerontologist*, 55(1): 26–33.

Katz, S., Down, T.D., Cash, H.R. and Grotz, R.C. (1970) 'Progress in the development of the index of ADL', *Gerontologist*, 10(1): 20–30.

King, R., Warnes, A.M. and Williams, A.M. (1998) 'International retirement migration in Europe', *International Journal of Population Geography*, 4(2): 91–111.

King, R., Warnes, T. and Williams, A. (2000) *Sunset Lives: British Retirement Migration to the Mediterranean*, Oxford: Berg.

King, R., Cela, E., Morettini, G. and Fokkema, T. (2019) 'The Marche: Italy's new frontier for international retirement migration', *Population, Space and Place*, 25(5): e2241. Available at: https://doi.org/10.1002/psp.2241 (accessed 23 July 2022).

King, R., Cela, E. and Fokkema, T. (2021) 'New frontiers in international retirement migration', *Ageing and Society*, 41(6): 1205–20.

Kosnick, K., Karacan, E. and Kahveci, C. (2021) 'Policy dimensions of retirement migration from Germany to the Turkish Riviera: comparing German and German-Turkish older migrants', in M. Repetti, T. Calasanti and C. Phillipson (eds) *Ageing and Migration in a Global Context*, Cham: Springer, pp 131–46.

Lain, D. (2012) 'Working past 65 in the UK and the USA: segregation into "Lopaq" occupations?', *Work, Employment and Society*, 26(1): 78–94.

Lain, D., Airey, L., Loretto, W. and Vickerstaff, S. (2019) 'Understanding older worker precarity: the intersecting domains of jobs, households and the welfare state', *Ageing and Society*, 39(19): 1–23.

Lain, D., Airey, L., Loretto, W. and Vickerstaff, S. (2021) 'Older workers and ontological precarity: between precarious employment, precarious welfare and precarious households', in A. Grenier, C. Phillipson and R. Settersten (eds) *Precarity and Ageing: Understanding Insecurity and Risk in Later Life*, Bristol: Policy Press, pp 91–114.

Lardiès-Bosque, R., Gullén, J.C. and Montes-de-Oca, V. (2016) 'Retirement migration and transnationalism in Northern Mexico', *Journal of Ethnic and Migration Studies*, 42(5): 816–33.

Lassus, L.A.P., Lopez, S. and Roscigno, V.J. (2015) 'Aging workers and the experience of job loss', *Research in Social Stratification and Mobility*, 41: 81–91.

Leimgruber, M. (2008) *Solidarity without the State? Business and the Shaping of the Swiss Welfare State: 1890–2000*, Cambridge: Cambridge University Press.

Leimgruber, M. (2013) 'La sécurité sociale au péril du vieillissement. Les organisations internationales et l'alarmisme démographique (1975–1995)', *Le Mouvement social*, 244: 31–45.

Levy, B.R. (2001) 'Eradication of ageism requires addressing the enemy within', *The Gerontologist*, 41(5): 578–9.

Levy, B.R. (2003) 'Mind matters: cognitive and physical effects of aging self-stereotypes', *Journals of Gerontology: Series B*, 58(4): P203–11.

Longino, C.F. and Biggar, J.C. (1981) 'The impact of retirement migration on the South', *The Gerontologist*, 21(3): 283–90.

Longino, C.F. and Bradley, D.E. (2006) 'Internal and international migration', in R.H. Binstock, L.K., George, S.J. Cutler, J. Hendricks and J.H. Schultz (eds) *Handbook of Aging and the Social Sciences*, Cambridge: Academic Press, pp 76–93.

Longino, C.F. and Marshall, V.W. (1990) 'North American research on seasonal migration', *Ageing and Society*, 10(2): 229–35.

Ma, A. and Chow, N.W.S. (2006) 'Economic impact of elderly amenity mobility in Southern China', *The Southern Gerontological Society*, 25(4): 275–90.

Macnicol, J. (2006) *Age Discrimination*, Cambridge: Cambridge University Press.

Macnicol, J. (2015) *Neoliberalising Old Age*, Cambridge: Cambridge University Press.

MacPherson, M., Smith-Lovin, L. and Cook, J.M. (2001) 'Birds of a feather: homophily in social networks', *Annual Review of Sociology*, 27: 415–44.

Madero-Cabib, I. (2016) 'The gendered and liberal retirement regime in Switzerland', in D. Hofäcker, M. Hess and S. König (eds) *Delaying Retirement*, London: Palgrave Macmillan, pp 269–90.

Mahfoudh, A., Waldis, B. and Kurt, S. (2021) 'Eldercare in transnational families and the Swiss immigration regime', in M. Repetti, T. Calasanti and C. Phillipson (eds) *Ageing and Migration in a Global Context: Challenges for Welfare States*, Cham: Springer, pp 65–79.

McHugh, K. (2000) 'The "ageless self"? Emplacement of identities in Sun Belt retirement communities', *Journal of Aging Studies*, 14(1): 103–15.

McMullin, J.A. and Berger, E.D. (2006) 'Gendered ageism/age(ed) sexism: the case of unemployed older workers', in T. Calasanti and K.F. Slevin (eds) *Age Matters: Realigning Feminist Thinking*, New York, NY: Routledge, pp 201–24.

Medicaid.gov (no date) Medicaid. Available at: www.medicaid.gov/medicaid/index.html (accessed 18 August 2022).

Medicare.gov (no date) Welcome to Medicare. Available at: www.medicare.gov (accessed 23 July 2022).

Miles, A. (2015) 'Health care imaginaries and retirement migration to Cuenca, Ecuador', *Journal of Latin American Geography*, 14(1): 39–55.

Minichiello, V., Browne, J. and Kendig, H. (2000) 'Perceptions and consequences of ageism: views of older people', *Ageing and Society*, 20(3): 253–78.

Murray, D. (2022) Healthcare in Mexico: overview of costs and plans available. Available at: https://internationalliving.com/countries/mexico/health-care/ (accessed 27 July 2022).

NHS (National Health Service) (2021) When the council might pay for your care. Available at: www.nhs.uk/conditions/social-care-and-support-guide/money-work-and-benefits/when-the-council-might-pay-for-your-care/ (accessed 23 July 2022).

NHS (2022) Benefits if you're over state pension age. Available at: www.nhs.uk/conditions/social-care-and-support-guide/money-work-and-benefits/benefits-if-you-are-over-state-pension-age/ (accessed 23 July 2022).

OECD (Organisation for Economic Co-operation and Development) (2022) OECD.Stat. Available at: https://stats.oecd.org/ (accessed 23 July 2022).

Olenski, A.R., Zimerman, A., Coussens, S. and Jenna, A.B. (2020) 'Behavioral heuristics in coronary-artery bypass graft surgery', *New England Journal of Medicine*, 382: 778–9.

Oliver, C. (2007) 'Imagined communitas: older migrants and aspirational mobility', in V. Amit (ed) *Going First Class? New Approaches to Privileged Travel and Movement*, New York, NY: Berghahn Books.

Oliver, C. (2008) *Retirement Migration: Paradoxes of Ageing*, Oxford: Routledge.

Oliver, C. (2017) 'Peer-led care practices and "community" formation in British retirement migration', *Nordic Journal of Migration Research*, 7(3): 172–80.

Ong, R., Wood, G.A., Cigdem-Bayram, M. and Salazar, S.M.S. (2019) *Precarious Home Ownership: Implications for Older Australians: AHURI Final Report No. 319*, Melbourne: Australian Housing and Urban Research Institute Limited. Available at: https://ssrn.com/abstract=3450192 (accessed 23 July 2022).

O'Reilly, K. (2000) *The British on the Costa del Sol: Trans-national Identities and Local Communities*, London: Routledge.

O'Reilly, K. (2007) 'Intra-European migration and the mobility – enclosure dialectic', *Sociology*, 41(2): 277–93.

Phillipson, C. (1998) *Reconstructing Old Age*, London: Sage.

Phillipson, C. (2007) 'The "elected" and the "excluded": sociological perspectives on the experience of place and community in old age', *Ageing and Society*, 27(3): 321–42.

Phillipson, C. (2019) '"Fuller" or "extended" working lives? Critical perspectives on changing transitions from work to retirement', *Ageing and Society*, 39(3): 629–50.

Phillipson, C. (2021) 'Austerity and precarity: individual and collective agency in later life', in A. Grenier, C. Phillipson and A. Sttersen (eds) *Precarity and Ageing: Understanding Insecurity and Risk in Later Life*, Bristol: Policy Press, pp 215–35.

Pickering, J., Crooks, V.A., Snyder, J. and Jeffery, M. (2019) 'What is known about the factors motivating short-term international retirement migration? A scoping review', *Population Ageing*, 12: 379–95.

Polivka, L. and Luo, B. (2021) 'From precarious employment to precarious retirement: neo-liberal health and long-term care in the United States', in A. Grenier, C. Phillipson and R.A. Settersten (eds) *Precarity and Ageing: Understanding Insecurity and Risk in Later Life*, Bristol: Policy Press, pp 191–213.

Rainer, G. (2019) 'Amenity/lifestyle migration to the Global South: driving forces and socio-spatial implications in Latin America', *Third World Quarterly*, 40(7): 1359–77.

Repetti, M. (2018) *Les Bonnes Figures de la Vieillesse*, Lausanne: Antipodes.

Repetti, M. and Bolzman, C. (2020) 'Ageing abroad: the case of Swiss nationals in Morocco and Spain', *Swiss Journal of Sociology*, 42(2): 199–217.

Repetti, M. and Calasanti, T. (2020) 'Retirement migration and transnational grandparental support: a Spanish case study', *Global Networks*, 20(2): 308–24.

Repetti, M. and Lawrence, J. (2021) 'The cultural and structural motivations of cheap mobility: the case of retirement migrants in Spain and Costa Rica', *Geoforum*, 124: 156–64.

Repetti, M. and Phillipson, C. (2020) 'Fin de carrière et vieillesse: deux facettes d'un même risque?', *Retraite et Société*, 48(2): 41–68.

Repetti, M. and Schilliger, S. (2021) 'In search of a good life in and out of Switzerland: making use of migration in old age', in M. Repetti, T. Calasanti and C. Phillipson (eds) *Ageing and Migration in a Global Context: Challenges for Welfare States*, Cham: Springer, pp 147–61.

Repetti, M., Phillipson, C. and Calasanti, T. (2018) 'Retirement migration: a choice for a better life?', *Sociological Research Online*, 23(4): 780–94.

Repetti, M., Calasanti, T. and Phillipson, C. (2021) 'Introduction', in M. Repetti, T. Calasanti and C. Phillipson (eds) *Ageing and Migration in a Global Context: Challenges for Welfare States*, Cham: Springer, pp 1–9.

Repetti, M., Mesnard, P., Fassa, F. and Harisson, K. (2022) 'Utile, mais pas indispensable?', *Gérontologie et Société*, 44(167): 173–88.

Rishworth, A. and Elliott, S. (2019) 'Global environmental change in an aging world: the role of space, place and scale', *Social Science and Medicine*, 227: 128–36.

Robb, C., Chen, H. and Haley, W.E. (2002) 'Ageism in mental health and health care: a critical review', *Journal of Clinical Geropsychology*, 8(1): 1–12.

Robin, A., Cha, A.E., Terlizzi, E.P. and Martinez, M.E. (2021) 'Demographic variation in health insurance coverage: United States, 2019', *National Health Statistics Reports*, 159: 1–16. Available at: www.cdc.gov/nchs/data/nhsr/nhsr159-508.pdf (accessed 16 August 2022).

Rocío Sáenz, M. and Acosta, J.L.B.M. (2010) *Universal Coverage in a Middle Income Country: Costa Rica*, Geneva: World Health Organization.

Rogne, L., Estes, C.L., Grossman, B.R., Hollister, B.A. and Solway, E. (2009) *Social Insurance and Social Justice, Social Security, Medicare, and the Campaign against Entitlements*, New York, NY: Springer.

Roll, J. (2009) *The Prescription Charge: Social Policy Section*, London: House of Common Library. Available at: https://tpauk.com/images/docs/the-prescription-charge-house-of-commons-library-2009.pdf (accessed 23 July 2022).

Roscigno, V.J., Mong, S., Byron, R. and Tester, G. (2007) 'Age discrimination, social closure and employment', *Social Forces*, 86(1): 313–34.

Sassen, S. (2000) 'Women's burden: counter-geographies of globalization and the feminization of survival', *Journal of International Affairs*, 53(2): 503–24.

Schilliger, S. (2015) 'Globalisierte Care-Arrangements in schweizer Privathaushalten', in M. Nollert and E. Nadai (eds) *Geschlechterverhältnisse im Post-Wohlfahrtsstaat*, Weinheim, Basel: Reihe Arbeitsgesellschaft im Wandel, Beltz Juventa, pp 154–75.

Schilt, K. (2006) 'Just one of the guys? How transmen make gender visible at work', *Gender and Society*, 20(4): 465–90.

Schweppe, C. (2022a) 'Falling through the net of social protection: the precarity of retirement migrants in Thailand', in C. Schweppe (ed) *Retirement Migration to the Global South: Global Inequalities and Entanglement*, Singapore: Palgrave Macmillan, pp 187–208.

Schweppe, C. (ed) (2022b) *Retirement Migration to the Global South: Global Inequalities and Entanglement*, Singapore: Palgrave Macmillan.

Schwiter, K., Berndt, C. and Truong, J. (2018) 'Neoliberal austerity and the marketisation of elderly care', *Social and Cultural Geography*, 19(3): 379–99.

Shah, S. (2020) *The Next Great Migration: The Story of Movement on a Changing Planet*, London: Bloomsbury.

Simmonds, B. (2021) *Ageing and the Crisis in Health and Social Care: Global and National Perspectives*, Bristol: Policy Press.

Sloane, P. and Silbersack, J. (2020) 'International retirement migration', in P. Sloane, S. Zimmerman and J. Silbersack (eds) *Retirement Migration from the U.S. to Latin American Colonial Cities*, Cham: Springer, pp 1–18.

Social Security Administration (2004) US – Mexican Social Security Agreement. Available at: www.ssa.gov/international/Agreement_Texts/mexico.html (accessed 23 July 2022).

Social Security Administration (2021) International programs. Available at: https://www.ssa.gov/international/payments.html (accessed February 21, 2023).

Sone, S. and Thang, L.L. (2020) 'Staying till the end? Japanese later-life migrants and belonging in Western Australia', *Japanese Studies*, 40(1): 41–62.

Strauss, S. (2021) 'Multiple engagement: the relationship between informal care-giving and formal volunteering among Europe's 50+ population', *Ageing and Society*, 41(7), 1562–86.

Sullivan, D.A. and Stevens, S.A. (1982) 'Snowbirds: seasonal migrants to the Sunbelt', *Research on Aging*, 4(2): 159–77.

Sullivan, L. and Meschede, T. (2016) 'Race, gender and senior economic well-being: how financial vulnerability over the life course shapes retirement for older women of color', *Public Policy & Aging Report*, 26(2): 58–62.

Sunanta, S. and Jaisuekun, K. (2022) 'Care as a right and care as a commodity: positioning international retirement migration in Thailand's old age care regime', in C. Schweppe (ed) *Retirement Migration to the Global South: Global Inequalities and Entanglements*, Singapore: Palgrave Macmillan.

Sunil, T.S., Rojas, V. and Bradley, D.E. (2007) 'United States' international retirement migration: the reasons for retiring to the environs of Lake Chapala, Mexico', *Ageing and Society*, 27(4): 489–510.

Swain, J., Carpentieri, J.D., Parsons, S. and Goodman, A. (2020) 'Approaching retirement after working life in poverty', *Journal of Population Ageing*, 1–21. Available at: https://doi.org/10.1007/s12062-020-09314-2 (accessed 23 July 2022).

Teh, B.C.G. (2018) 'Retirement migration: the Malaysia my Second Home (MM2H) program and the Japanese retirees in Penang', *International Journal of Asia Pacific Studies*, 14(1): 79–106.

Timonen, V. (2016) *Beyond Successful and Active Ageing: A Theory of Model Ageing*, Bristol: Policy Press.

Torres, S. (2012) 'International migration: patterns and implications for exclusion in old age', in T. Scharf and N.C. Keating (eds) *From Exclusion to Inclusion in Old Age*, Bristol: Policy Press, pp 33–49.

Torres, S. (2019) *Ethnicity and Old Age: Expanding our Imagination*, Bristol: Policy Press.

Townsend, J., Godfrey, M. and Denby, T. (2006) 'Heroines, villains, and victims: older people's perceptions of others', *Ageing and Society*, 26(6): 883–900.

Tremlett, G. (2006) *Ghosts of Spain*, London: Faber and Faber Limited.

Tulin, M., Volker, B. and Lancee, B. (2021) 'The same place but different: how neighborhood context differentially affects homogeneity in networks of different social groups', *Journal of Urban Affairs*, 43(1): 57–76.

UN (United Nations) (2016) *International Migration Report*. New York: United Nations.

UN (2019) International migration 2019: wall chart. Available at: www.un.org/en/development/desa/population/migration/publications/wallchart/docs/MigrationStock2019_Wallchart.pdf (accessed 23 July 2022).

UN (2022) Global issues: migration. Available at: www.un.org/en/global-issues/migration (accessed 23 July 2022).

Waldinger, R. and Fitzgerald, D. (2004) 'Transnationalism in question', *American Journal of Sociology*, 109(5): 1117–95.

Walker, A. and Foster, L. (2006) 'Caught between virtue and ideological necessity. A century of pension policies in the UK', *Review of Political Economy*, 18(3): 427–48.

Warburton, J., Hung Ng, S. and Sharlow, S.M. (2013) 'Social inclusion in an ageing world: introduction to the special issue', *Ageing and Society*, 33(1): 1–15.

Warnes, A.M. (1993) 'The development of retirement migration in Great Britain', *Space Populations Societies*, 3: 451–64.

Williams, A.M., King, R., Warnes, A. and Patterson, G. (2000) 'Tourism and international retirement migration: new forms of an old relationship in Southern Europe', *Tourism Geographies*, 2(1): 28–49.

Williamson, J. and Béland, D. (2015) 'The future of retirement security in comparative perspective', in L. George and K. Ferraro (eds) *Handbook of Aging and the Social Sciences*, Cambridge: Academic Press, pp 461–81.

Woodspring, N. (2016) *Baby Boomers: Time and Ageing Bodies*, Bristol: Policy Press.

Wyman, M.F., Shiovitz-Ezra, S. and Bengel, J. (2018) 'Ageism in the health care system: providers, patients, and systems', in L. Ayalon and C. Tesch-Römer (eds) *Contemporary Perspectives on Ageism*, Cham: Springer, pp 193–212.

Index

A

active/successful ageing 16, 23, 121, 122
activities of daily living (ADLs) 9, 19, 21, 32, 34, 45, 104, 113, 123
adventure seeking 85–6, 90
Affordable Care Act (US, 2010) 36–7
ageing in place 15
ageism
　'burden' of older people 9, 23, 27, 36, 68–78, 122
　care needs 110
　devaluation 6–7, 22–4, 69–78, 105
　escaping 67–88
　health precarity 106
　in healthcare 9, 22, 116, 123
　internalised 84, 87
　labour markets 23, 47–8, 120
　and precarity 6–7, 13, 27, 128
　and retirement migration 22–4
　social exclusion 44, 121–2
　in workplace 49, 51
Ahmed, A. 119
amenity-related motivations 3, 19
anti-ageing industry 7, 23, 68
anti-poverty policies 42
Asia, as destination 14
assets 31, 44, 50, 65, 124–5
assistance 9, 104–17, 122–4, 125–6
　see also activities of daily living (ADLs); care needs/care purchasing; instrumental activities for daily living (IADLs)
assisted living 112
augmenting income while retired 53, 54, 63, 90
austerity 7, 13, 19–20, 30, 33, 91, 128
autonomy 27, 68, 117

B

back-and-forth migration 5
banking fees 43
bedroom communities 82
Béland, D. 23, 29, 30, 35, 36, 39
belonging 78–83, 87
Bender, D. 9, 14, 21, 92, 119
Benson, M. 14, 15, 16, 19, 20, 64, 92, 93, 99, 103, 118, 129
blended families 7, 45
Bolzman, C. 14, 17, 21, 91
border arrangements 17, 91–2, 95
Botterill, K. 20, 21, 22
Brexit 20, 31, 43, 60, 64, 82, 93, 126, 129

'burden' of older people 9, 23, 27, 36, 68–78, 122
Butler, R.N. 6, 22

C

Calasanti, T. 6, 7, 8, 9, 14, 17, 18, 22, 23, 24, 29, 36, 39, 44, 68, 73, 106, 111, 122
Calzada, I. 13
capitalism 29, 120
　see also neoliberalism
care needs/care purchasing
　barriers to accessing in host country 21
　care precarity 9, 104–17, 122–4, 125–6
　family-based care 21, 71, 110
　global care chain 19
　global power relations and migration 92
　informal care 9, 18, 19
　live-in caregivers 112–13
　long-term care needs 21, 23, 32, 34, 37–8, 107, 111–16, 122–4, 127
　loving care 109–10, 114–15, 116–17
　quality of care 113, 114–15
　Switzerland 34
　UK 32
　unpaid care work 19, 23
　see also activities of daily living (ADLs); assistance; instrumental activities for daily living (IADLs); women
care work 23, 32, 56, 58, 92
charitable organisations 32, 76–8, 99, 103, 129
children, supporting 55, 56
Ciafone, A. 4, 18, 20, 24, 27, 42, 85, 122
citizenship 21, 92–4
class 4, 8, 69, 79
cold weather, escaping 2
colonialism 13, 18, 92, 93, 96
communication technology 15, 18
community of 'alikes' 78–83
community service 23, 76–8
　see also voluntary work
consumers, retirement migrants as 75, 120
Costa Rica
　airports 95
　attitudes towards older people 69–70, 71, 86
　availability of assistance 112, 115–16
　citizenship 93–4
　cost of travel 59
　global inequalities 97
　healthcare access 93, 100, 107–8, 125
　language 99
　local community, contributing to 76
　local economy, contributing to 75

146

Index

as location of research 24–5, 26
migrant communities 78, 79, 80–1, 87
migrants' access to welfare state policies 42–3
retirement migrants as source of foreign currency 75
voluntary work 99
COVID-19 24–5, 99, 105
crime, fear of 73
Croucher, S. 27, 57, 104, 108, 109, 111, 112, 115, 120, 122, 129
cultural identities 14, 16

D

dating 82
de São José, J.M.S. 6, 8, 22
debts, reducing 54, 67
deference 70–1, 86, 100, 103, 111
dental care 1, 30, 34, 45, 61, 107, 125
dependent family members 7
devaluation 6–7, 22–4, 69–78, 105
disability 56
discrimination 6, 7
see also ageism
divorce 7, 45, 46, 50, 51, 52, 55, 124
domestic staff, hiring local 75, 97

E

early retirement 5, 33, 50, 51–4, 62, 120, 124–5
economic precarity 20, 46–66, 119–21, 128
Ecuador 20, 72–3, 75, 98, 108–9, 116, 122
elite phenomenon, retirement migration as 4
energy costs 50, 59, 60
English-speaking 99, 103
environmental concerns 96
equity 124–5
Estes, C.L. 23, 28, 36, 38, 124
Eur-Lex 42
European Union (EU) 17, 42, 43, 60, 93
exchange rates 60, 89, 98
'expats' terminology 3–4
exploitation 96–9, 122, 129–30

F

family links 15–16, 17–18, 55, 56, 89, 90, 94–6
family-based care 21, 71, 110
fear of crime 73
Fine, M. 9, 109, 118, 122
Fitzgerald, D. 91
flights, availability/cost of 15, 17, 59, 92, 94–6, 103
food costs 50, 59, 60
frailty 6, 109–10

friends 55, 79, 85
see also social networks
frugal living 53–4

G

Gambold, L. 16, 20, 21, 27, 42
gated communities 73
Gavanas, A. 13, 19, 42
gentrification 15, 19
geopolitical privilege 18, 20
Glenn, E.N. 110, 111, 113
global care chain 19
global privileges 89–103, 116
global relations 3–4, 15, 18–19, 110–11, 115, 116, 123, 129–30
globalisation 5, 110–11, 118, 128
grandparents 18, 90, 95
Grenier, A. 5, 6, 7, 8, 13, 14, 44, 109–10, 118
gringo pricing 100, 101, 103, 124
growth in retirement migration 2–4
guilt/regret about moving 64
Guo, H.J. 9

H

Hall, K. 8, 9, 17, 18, 20, 21, 22, 105, 109, 110, 119, 122, 127
Hardill, I. 4, 15, 17, 18, 20, 21, 22
Hayes, M. 13, 16, 19, 20, 27, 72, 75, 85, 92–3, 97, 98, 100, 101, 118, 120–1, 122
health as social construction 105–9
health insurance
  Costa Rica 107
  history 5
  lack of 21, 122–3
  migrants' access to welfare state policies 42–3
  neoliberalism 39, 40–1, 45
  private health insurance 21, 31, 33–4, 35, 36–8, 39, 60, 106
  Spain 43
  Switzerland 33–4, 61, 125
  USA 8, 28–9, 35, 36–8, 62, 93–4, 106
  see also Medicaid; Medicare
health policies
  ageism 9
  as motivation for migration 8–9, 122–4
  and neoliberalism 38–42
  Switzerland 33–5, 40–1, 44–5, 125
  UK 30–2, 40–1, 44–5, 125
  USA 36–8, 40–1, 44–5, 125
health precarity 8–9, 104–17, 122–4
healthcare access
  ageism 22, 116, 123
  British migrants in Spain 59–60, 63, 64
  'healthcare refugees' 19, 20, 106–7
  in home country 17, 59, 93–4, 112
  hope of reduced costs 50–1

international agreements 93
medical tourism 107, 109
Mexico 89
migrants' access to welfare state
  policies 42–3
  as motivation for migration 9, 20–1, 50–1
  and neoliberalism 38–42
  post-Brexit EU 60, 64, 93
  prices for migrants versus locals 100
  quality of healthcare 106–7, 108–9
  Swiss migrants in Spain 61, 63
  UK 30–2
  US migrants' cost of living 62–3, 90
hearing care 30, 34, 45, 116, 125
home adaptations 112–13, 114
home country, return to 4, 16–17, 18, 21, 59, 94–5
home ownership 46, 50, 55, 65
hosting family 18
household compositions 7, 45, 50, 58
  see also divorce
household staff, hiring local 75, 97
housing costs 50, 60, 61, 64
Huber, A. 14
Hunter, A. 92
Hurd, L. 85

I

ill health 52, 53, 54, 104–17
  see also disability; frailty; healthcare access
income supplementation 53, 54, 63, 90
independence, maintaining 90
individualism 16, 29, 30, 38–9
inequality
  awareness of 67
  colonialism 13
  global relations 18–19, 96–102, 109, 129
  between home and host country 42
  intersecting systems of 39, 49
  labour markets 29
  privilege 91–2
  reproduced in pension system 32, 33
  between retirement migrants 20
  US 38
  see also ageism
inflation 29, 32
informal care 9, 18, 19
informal staff 75
information gathering 59
instrumental activities for daily living (IADLs) 9, 21, 34, 39, 45, 104, 113
insurance policies 5, 21, 29, 32, 40–1
  see also health insurance
integration in host society 13–14, 75, 78, 82, 87, 98, 101
intergenerational wealth transfers 23
international agreements 17, 42, 45, 92–3
international communities 81
International Living 1, 3, 56–7, 59, 104

International Organisation for Migration 2–3
Internet access 18, 92
intersectionality 24, 69
interview methods 24–5
invisibility 67, 68, 69, 83, 86

J

Jaisuekun, K. 120
job insecurity 48–9

K

Kalleberg, A.L. 49
Katz, S. 9
King, R. 4, 5, 7, 14, 15, 16, 17, 23, 106

L

labour markets
  ageism 23, 47–8, 120
  difficulty in finding jobs 52
  insecurity 49
  instability 5
  marginalisation of older workers 6
  'not in the labour force' older people 50, 51–2
  staying employed until retirement age 54–6
Lain, D. 5, 6, 7, 8, 13, 30, 45, 49–50, 51, 53, 54, 58, 118, 119, 128
language 9, 21, 26, 99, 122
Lassus, L.A.P. 6, 8, 22, 23, 51, 52
Lawrence, J. 17, 18, 96, 103
legal status 21
  see also citizenship; residency
Levy, B.R. 68, 84
liberalism 29, 39
  see also neoliberalism
lifestyle-related motivations 3, 15–16
live-in caregivers 112–13
living with other migrants 78–83
local communities, contributing to 76–8, 86–7, 97, 98–9, 103
local economies, impact on 18–19, 74–6, 86–7, 92, 96–8, 117, 120, 129
local workers, hiring 18–19, 97, 101–2, 110–11, 113–15, 117, 122, 129
locations of research 24–5
long-term care needs 21, 23, 32, 34, 37–8, 107, 111–16, 122–4, 127
loving care 109–10, 114–15, 116–17
Luo, B. 128

M

Macnicol, J. 7, 23, 128
means-tested benefits 30, 32, 35
Medicaid 37–8, 41, 90, 93–4
medical tourism 107, 109
Medicare 28–9, 37, 38, 40, 43, 45, 62, 90, 106, 107, 108, 116, 125
men, invisibility of 72–4

Mexico
  assistance facilities for older people 111–12
  attitudes towards older people 69–70, 71–2, 86
  care systems 104
  citizenship 94
  fear of crime 73
  global privileges 89
  gringo pricing 100, 101, 103, 124
  healthcare access 107, 125
  integration 101–2
  language 99
  locals' attitudes towards migrants 100
  as location of research 24–5, 26
  migrant communities of older people 79–80, 81–2, 84, 87
  migrants' access to welfare state policies 42–3
  part-time migrants 82
  quality of care 114–15
  as site of research 20
  travel to/from 59, 95
  unpredictable/dynamic precarity 126–7
  visibility 74
  voluntary work 77
middle classes 19
Miles, A. 19, 92, 106, 108–9, 116, 120, 127
mixed-age communities, preferences for 84–5
Morocco 14
mortgages 50, 55, 61, 67
motivations for migration
  amenity-related motivations 3, 19
  health-related 8–9, 20–1, 50–1, 122–4
  lifestyle-related motivations 3, 15–16
  and precarity 19–22, 118–30
  research on migration 14–15
  unemployment 51–2, 120, 121
  weather 2, 13, 59
  welfare state policies 19–20, 125–6
Murray, D. 104

N

National Health Service (UK) 28, 30–1
neighbourhoods, changing 15
neighbours, knowing 81, 82
  see also local communities, contributing to
neoliberalism 5, 7, 13, 19–20, 38–42, 58, 91, 110–11, 119
'not in the labour force' older people 50, 51–2
nursing homes 111, 113

O

OECD (Organisation for Economic Co-operation and Development) 30, 31, 33, 34, 38
Oliver, C. 14, 15, 17, 18, 20, 22, 87
ontological consequences 8

O'Reilly, K. 14, 15, 16, 20, 87
outsiders, migrants as 100, 101, 124
'outsourcing' older people 27, 42, 112, 122

P

partner, loss of 21
  see also divorce
part-time migrants 4–5, 13, 16
part-time residents 82
pensions
  2007–08 financial crisis 57
  access abroad 42–4
  British migrants in Spain 59–60
  early claiming of 51, 52–4
  economic precarity 21, 23, 29, 39, 57
  global inequalities 97
  income gap from end of work 7
  migrants' access to welfare state policies 42–3
  neoliberalism 39, 124
  private pensions 30, 32–3, 35–6, 124
  state pension eligibility age 30, 33, 36, 38
  Switzerland 32–3, 40–1
  UK 29–30, 40–1
  USA 35–6, 40–1, 61–3
perpetual tourists 93–4
personal care 9, 31, 34, 39
  see also care needs/care purchasing
personal safety 73–4
personhood, maintenance of 9, 68
Phillipson, C. 5, 6, 7, 8, 14, 15, 16, 19, 23, 24, 29, 38, 42, 49, 128
Polivka, L. 128
postcolonialism 18, 92, 99, 105, 118
poverty
  comparative table 31
  Pension Credit (UK) 30
  poverty-reduction policies 28–9
  Switzerland 31, 33
  UK 30, 31
  USA 31, 36, 37–8, 39
  women 29, 33, 39
power
  colonialism 13, 18, 92, 93, 96
  global inequalities 96–102, 103
  Global North-South 3–4, 92
  global power relations and migration 15, 18–19, 110–11, 115, 116, 123, 129–30
  global privileges 89–103, 116
  postcolonialism 18, 92, 99, 105, 118
  and wealth 102
precarity, defined 5–9, 14
prescription drugs 30, 37–8, 40–1, 43
private health insurance 21, 31, 33–4, 35, 36–8, 39, 60, 106
private pensions 30, 32–3, 35–6, 124
privilege 68, 85, 89–103, 118, 123–4, 129

R

Rainer, G. 15, 19
recession 2007–8 56–8, 119, 124
redundancy/severance 48, 49, 51, 52
reinvention of self 16
remarriage 47, 50
remote working 89
Repetti, M. 7, 8, 14, 17, 18, 20, 21, 23, 29, 42, 92, 96, 103
research before choosing a location to migrate to 59
residency 21, 43, 64, 93, 107
respect for older people 67, 69–72, 88, 101, 112, 121–2
retirement age 30, 33, 36, 38, 54–6
rooms, renting out 54
RV living 46

S

safety 73–4, 86
Sapra, A. 9
savings 50, 56, 57, 119, 124
Schengen Agreement 93
Schilliger, S. 92
Schweppe, C. 14, 17, 21, 22, 92, 122, 127
seasonal migration 5, 13, 16
self-employment 58, 89, 90
selling houses bought as a migrant 64
severance pay 48, 49, 51, 52
Silbersack, J. 5, 43
Simmonds, B. 5, 8, 32, 39, 104
single people 20, 51
single women 16, 51, 63, 64, 65–6, 73–4, 127
Sloane, P. 5, 43
social care 31–2, 34, 104
social class 4, 8, 69, 79
social cohesion 18, 23
social inclusion/exclusion 8, 23–4, 44, 68–9, 76–8, 96–9, 103, 121–4
social justice 129
social networks 18, 79, 81, 110
social participation 76–8
social precarity 68–9, 86, 121–2, 127
Spain
  2007–08 financial crisis 57
  attitudes towards older people 69–71, 86
  availability of care services 21, 110
  British retirement migrants 5, 99
  as favoured destination 14
  healthcare access 125
  local economy, contributing to 75
  as location of research 24–6
  migrant communities of older people 78, 81, 82–3, 87
  migrants' access to welfare state policies 42–3
  safety 74
  travel 59, 94
  voluntary work 76
Spanish, learning 99
state pension eligibility age 30, 33, 36, 38
statistics
  British retirement migrants 5
  international migration 2–3
stereotypes 6, 16, 22
Stevens, S.A. 14
successful/active ageing 16, 23, 121, 122
Sullivan, D.A. 14
Sunanta, S. 120
supplementary incomes 53, 54, 63, 90
sustainability 96
Switzerland
  health policies 40–1, 44–5, 106, 125
  international agreements 42–3
  living costs 61
  pensions 32–3, 40–1, 124
  poverty 31, 33
  research on migration 14
  retirement age 54
  welfare state policies for later life 28–9, 32–5

T

taxes 1, 31, 32–3, 35, 58, 60, 93, 100
temporary migration 5, 13
Thailand 14, 21, 95
tourism industry 15, 93
tourist visas 5
transnational ageing 92
transnationalism 91–6, 103
travel, ease/cost of 15, 16–17, 59, 92, 94–6, 103
Tremlett, G. 99

U

UK
  health policies 30–2, 40–1, 44–5, 125
  living costs 59–60
  migration for healthcare reasons 20
  pensions 29–30, 40–1
  poverty 30, 31
  research on migration 14
  welfare state policies for later life 28–9
unemployment
  ageism 23
  long-term 7–8
  as reason for migration 51–2, 120, 121
  risks of 49
unpaid care work 19, 23
unpredictable/dynamic precarity 126–8, 129
USA
  attitudes to older people 70
  health policies 36–8, 40–1, 44–5, 89, 106–7, 125
  healthcare access 104
  'healthcare refugees' 19, 20, 106–7

international agreements 93
living costs 61–3
pensions 35–6, 40–1
poverty 31, 36, 39
research on migration 13–14
retirement at pension age 55
retirement migrant statistics 5
welfare state policies for later life 28–9, 35–8
working beyond retirement age 45

V

value of older lives 69–78, 106
see also ageism; devaluation
visas 21, 93
visibility 69–78
see also invisibility
vision care 30, 34, 45, 61, 107, 116, 125
voluntary work 76–8, 99, 103, 129

W

Waldinger, R. 91
'warehousing' older people 112
warmer climate, moving for 2, 13
weather 2, 13, 59
welfare state policies 28–45
  daily assistance 9
  health precarity 106, 124–6
  healthcare access 8–9
  international agreements 17
  and labour market insecurity 49
  and later-life precarity 7, 128–9
  motivations for migration 19–20, 125–6
  neoliberalism 58
  Switzerland 32–5
  UK 29–32
  USA 35–8, 90
  see also health insurance; pensions
welfare state retrenchment 5
widowhood 21
Williamson, J. 23, 29, 30, 35, 36, 39
winter, migration for 13
within-nation migration 4
women
  ageism 24, 69
  as carers 21, 32, 34, 56, 58, 92, 109, 110–11, 113–15, 127
  economic precarity 20, 51, 63, 64–5
  invisibility 72–4
  migration as escape from precarity 20
  as 'natural' caregivers 111, 115
  poverty 29, 33, 39
  precarious employment 8
  retirement age 33
  return to home country after death of partner 21
  single women 16, 51, 63, 64, 65–6, 73–4, 127
  voluntary work 77
working beyond retirement age 7, 42, 45, 47, 50
working classes 8
working conditions, precarious 46–9

Y

young people, wanting to live near 84–5, 122
youth, privileging of 6–7
  see also ageism

www.ingramcontent.com/pod-product-compliance
Lightning Source LLC
Chambersburg PA
CBHW071713020426
42333CB00017B/2249